Joyful Health

A 12-Week Biblical Workbook For Intuitive Eating And Exercising

Written by

Aubrey Golbek & Kasey Shuler

Cover design by Mattox Shuler

Cover photo by Dwayne Golbek

Interior formatting by Aubrey Golbek

Icons made by freepik from www.flaticon.com

ISBN: 9798668248063

Dedication

This book is dedicated to our clients: past, present, and future. Thank you for stepping out in faith to find greater joy in your relationship with food, fitness and body.

Contents

Introduction

Dear Friend,

If you've picked up this journal and signed up for the Joyful Health course, we have to assume you're in pursuit of more than calorie counting and fitness trends, that what you're really after is joy—joy in your relationship with food and body, and joy in your soul! If that's you, if you're searching for health that endures longer than the fad diets and goes deeper than physical appearance, then come to the well, dear one. True health is found in Jesus, in beholding God's unending, unmerited love and favor poured out for us—His grace!

Weekly Journal Questions

This journal was created as a companion to our 12-week online course, designed to help you discover a natural, healthy relationship with food and exercise. In it, you will find questions and worksheets that will assist you as you dive deeper into the concepts we discuss in each week's videos.

Chapters are divided by week, questions are broken up into "Eat Well" and "Move Free" sections, and further divided by the video they relate to. You will get the most out of the journaling experience if you watch one teaching video before completing its corresponding questions.

After the week's journal questions, you will find a "By Grace" section. The blank space in this section is for you to pray and reflect with the Lord on what you are learning throughout the week. It can also be used as a space to take notes while you watch the videos.

Joyful Health at a Glance Calendars

We've included three blank "Joyful Health at a Glance" calendars, one before weeks 1-4, another before weeks 5-8, and a final one before weeks 9-12. Use this space to plan your month ahead of time. You might choose to write down when you will watch each week's teaching video, the date and time of live trainings if you're doing the group coaching track, or when to check in with your partner. You might also use it to plan out workout days, rest days, and grocery shopping days, or to pencil in upcoming life events, weekly objectives or goal markers. It's yours to use however you please!

Menu Sketch

Please use the menu sketch page at the beginning of each week to roughly plan out a week of eating. In Week 10 we discuss "Meal Planning Without Rigidity" in detail, but for the majority of the course, simply use the space to brainstorm meal and snack ideas and prepare a grocery list. There is no need to craft a strict meal plan and follow it to a T. Instead, we want to offer you a tool to make eating easier. You decide what is useful and life-giving for you!

Exercise Ideas

The weekly exercise ideas page is your space to jot down ways you would like to exercise during the week. If it helps you with logistics, fill in the space provided with your specific plans. Make sure to schedule same muscle group strength sessions on non-consecutive days and include an active rest day. We will talk more about creating your exercise plan in Week 2. You may use the FITT recommendations provided on page 6 of the introduction to guide you, but feel free to change it up based on your body and day's needs. Let the voice of God's love lead you!

Daily Tracking Sheets

Below the weekly menu and exercise ideas sheet you will find three daily tracking pages. Here at Joyful Health, we believe eating well and moving freely starts with grace and ends with joy. For this reason, each daily page starts with Scripture and is followed by gratitude to help us turn our eyes to grace and shift our hearts to joy. We also believe that God designed our bodies with care, placing within them internal cues for regulating hunger and fullness, cravings to signal nutritional needs, and taste buds to provide enjoyment in eating. On each daily tracking sheet there is space for tracking food intake and for rating hunger, fullness, and satisfaction. Please refer to the hunger and fullness guide on page 5 of the Introduction for assistance with choosing a rating.

Below the food section, you will find a space to note movement practices. This includes a table to record what you need from movement, the time of day, the workout you chose, and how you felt before and afterwards. You may include physical feelings like increased energy, emotional feelings of peace, or spiritual feelings of freedom. Document the details and become an expert of your own experience. Reference the "Fitness Felt Need" chart on page 6 of the Introduction for guidance.

Finally, at the bottom of each daily tracking page is a prompt for noting other self-care practices and a space for recording what God is teaching you through the tracking experience. Use this final question to reflect on what is and is not life-giving for you, to uncover what God is teaching you through this process, or to problem solve for future days. This journey of getting to know your body and trusting God with food and movement is trial and error, experiment and discovery, so don't skip this part!

Exercise Tracking Sheet

Use the Exercise Tracking Sheet if you plan on sticking with a set of exercises to mark your progress. There are spaces to jot down the weight you use, repetitions, sets, as well as Rate of Perceived Exertion (RPE) on a scale of 1-10, described below in terms of your ability to breathe during movement:

1	Very light activity: Can sing easily
2-3	Light activity: Can carry on conversation
4-6	Moderate activity: Can carry short conversations
7-8	Vigorous activity: Can speak a sentence
9	Very Hard: Can speak a word
10	Max Effort: Unable to speak

Include notes on cardio activity: how long, how far, and how hard you exercise.

A Final Note on How to Use this Journal

"It is for freedom Christ has set you free. Stand firm, therefore, and do not submit again to a yoke of slavery." Galatians 5:1

We are so thankful you have decided to join us on this journey together! This is a beautiful time of renewal, a chance to step away from external guides, an opportunity to listen and lean in to the Lord's voice and allow Him to form you in His love, rather than conforming to the image of the world.

This journal was crafted with your freedom in mind. It doesn't have to be a checklist item to be completed with pride, or a chore to be avoided with guilt. The *Joyful Health Journal* is simply a tool at your disposal to connect with how God designed your body to eat and move.

Some days, you may choose to track your intake and rate your hunger and fullness, and some days, you may choose not to. There is no right or wrong way to use this journal. We believe food tracking and getting to know your body's needs is a short-term endeavor, much like taking a college course or learning how to ride a bike. Once you have the hang of it, you will likely only need to brush up every now and then.

We hope *The Joyful Health Journal* serves as a launching pad to a more joyful, Spirit-led relationship with food and movement. Most of all, we pray it helps you connect deeply with the Holy Spirit and the body God gave you. Nobody else is made like you, and we are looking forward to hearing how God is setting you free to be you, fully alive in Him!

May you have greater freedom with food, movement, and your body. May your joy in the Lord continue to increase!

grace & joy,
Aubrey and Kasey

Hunger & Fullness Scale

 Starving, feeling lightheaded, dizzy, extreme hunger.

 Starting to fill up, but not uncomfortable, feel like you could definitely eat more.

 Very hungry, irritable and anxious, feelings of wanting to eat everything in sight.

 Full, no longer hungry, but not uncomfortably full.

 Hungry, but not uncomfortable, clear physical symptoms of hunger.

 Very full, feel like you could go five hours without getting hungry again, might want to nap.

 Starting to feel hungry. Thinking about food, having some physical symptoms, able to wait a little bit to eat.

 Feeling very stuffed and uncomfortable.

 Neutral, not hungry and not full.

 Feeling sick you are so full.

Plate Examples

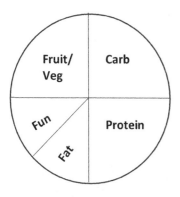

Meal Template

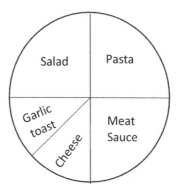

Lasagna Dinner

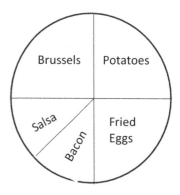

Breakfast Hash

FITT Guide

	Frequency	Intensity	Time	Type
STRENGTH	2-3 / week	Perform each set until muscle fatigue	2-3 sets of 4-15 repetitions for each major muscle group	Include all major muscle groups: legs, chest, back, biceps, triceps, shoulders, core
CARDIO	3-5 / week	Exert 60-90% effort	20-60 minutes / session	Include all planes of motion
STRETCH / MOBILITY	2-7 / week	Stretch to full range of motion without pain	15-30 seconds / stretch	Include all major muscle groups

Fitness Felt Need Guide

Root Need	Physical Indicators	Workout Suggestion	Spiritual Intention
CONFIDENCE	Slumped neck and shoulders, hands in pockets, limbs crossed	Master a small strength /speed challenge in an inspirational setting	"All things in Christ"
STRESS RELIEF	Shallow breathing, fidgety, headaches	Move to music, get outside, direct attention to your breath	Inhale "Jesus", exhale "sets me free"
TO BE FIT AND READY	Fatigue with normal activity, inability to focus	Timed compound interval workouts ~ 75% intensity	"Filled with the Father's finished work"
TO FEEL ALIVE	Muscle tension, restlessness, cravings for warmth	Invite a friend, conquer a challenge	"His victory lap!"
TO FEEL BETTER	Aches and pains hindering daily life	Stretch, walk, prehab and rehab exercises	"God is faithful"

Getting Started

Why did you sign up for this course?

What is your hope for the end of this course?

Eat Well

🎥 The Problem with Dieting and Food Rules

"Do not be conformed to this world, but be transformed by the renewal of your mind, that by testing you may discern what is the will of God, what is good and acceptable and perfect." Romans 12:2

After watching the video, "The Problem with Dieting and Food Rules," take time to answer these questions:

What diets have you been on in the past? Think about your dieting history beginning with your first diet and ending with your most recent diet. What motivated you to begin each diet, what were the "rules," what were the short-term results, and ultimately what were the long-term results?

What did you like about any of these diets?

What impact have they made on your relationship with food and body today?

Which, if any, of the side effects of dieting mentioned in the video have you experienced?

Why do you want to do things differently this time around?

Tell God what you need and ask him to do far better than you could imagine in your relationship with food and body. Journal your prayer below.

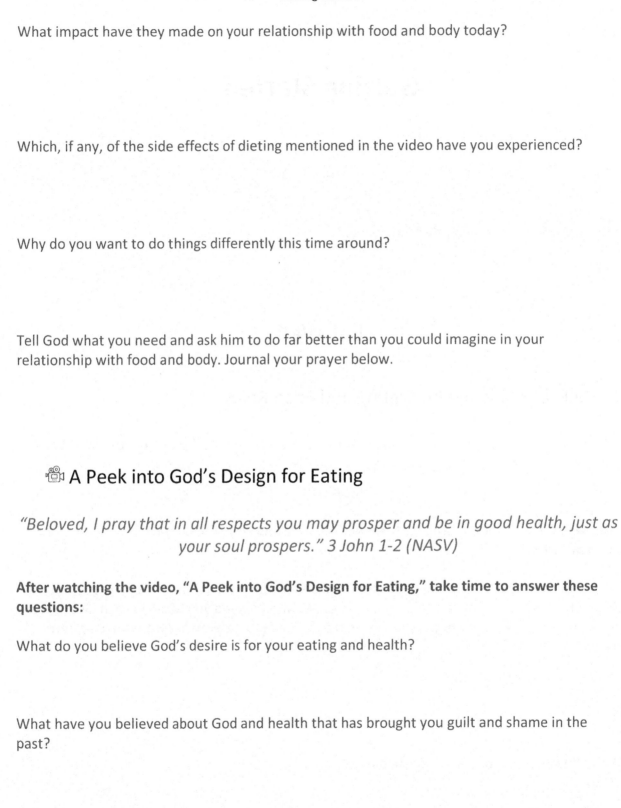 A Peek into God's Design for Eating

"Beloved, I pray that in all respects you may prosper and be in good health, just as your soul prospers." 3 John 1-2 (NASV)

After watching the video, "A Peek into God's Design for Eating," take time to answer these questions:

What do you believe God's desire is for your eating and health?

What have you believed about God and health that has brought you guilt and shame in the past?

Has God changed your heart in these areas? When? How?

What questions/concerns do you have about intuitive eating and how it fits with God's word/desires for you? (feel free to ask these in the live Facebook chat)

Move Free

🎥 Exercise is Not Punishment

"There is no fear in love, but perfect love casts out fear. For fear has to do with punishment, and whoever fears has not been perfected in love." 1 John 4:18

After watching the video, "Exercise is Not Punishment," take time to answer these questions:

What is your history and relationship with exercise?

How do you feel expected to exercise?

Think about the fitness or weight loss program that has most impacted you, and write down answers to the following:

    a. What are you seeing?

    b. What are they saying?

    c. What are they selling?

    d. What are you thinking?

If you avoid exercise, what are you afraid of?

Do you ever exercise out of fear, like the fear that you'll gain weight or develop a chronic disease?

What does exercise have to do with being perfected in love (see also Hebrews 2:10)?

🎥 Choosing to Move for the Joy of the Lord

"...[T]he joy of the Lord is our strength" Nehemiah 8:10

After watching "Choosing to Move for the Joy of the Lord," take time answer these questions:

What is the main reason you workout?

Is this reason from fear or out of love?

Are there any workouts that feel like a chore or painful? Do you feel the freedom to step away from them for a time?

Do you believe God will love you more if you exercise more, or less if you don't exercise at all? Has being an "exerciser" or a "person who doesn't like fitness" become part of your identity?

By Grace

Lord, thank you for teaching me...

MONTH OF: _____

Joyful Health at a Glance

SUN	MON	TUES	WED	THURS	FRI	SAT

Week One

Eat Well

🎥 Assessing Your Relationship with Food

"For by the grace given to me I say to everyone among you not to think of himself more highly than he ought to think, but to think with sober judgment, each according to the measure of faith that God has assigned." Romans 12:3

After watching the video, "Assessing Your Relationship with Food," take time to complete this assessment and answer the questions that follow:

Intuitive Eating Self-Assessment

Yes/No	Section 1: Unconditional Permission to Eat
	1. I try to avoid certain foods high in fat, carbs or calories.
	2. If I am craving a certain food, I don't allow myself to have it.
	3. I get mad at myself for eating something unhealthy.
	4. I have forbidden foods that I don't allow myself to eat.
	5. I don't allow myself to eat what food I desire at the moment.

Yes/No	
	6. I follow eating rules or diet plans that dictate what, when and/or how to eat.
Yes/No	**Section 2. Eating for Physical Rather than Emotional Reasons**
	1. I find myself eating when I'm feeling emotional (anxious, sad, depressed), even when I'm not physically hungry.
	2. I find myself eating when I am lonely, even when I'm not physically hungry.
	3. I use food to help me sooth my negative emotions.
	4. I find myself eating when I am stressed out, even when I'm not physically hungry.
	5. I am unable to cope with my negative emotions (i.e. anxiety and sadness) without turning to food for comfort.
	6. When I am bored, I eat just for something to do.
	7. When I am lonely, I turn to food for comfort.
	8. I have difficulty finding ways to cope with stress and anxiety, other than by eating.

Yes/No	
Yes/No	**Section 3. Reliance on Internal Hunger/Satiety Cues (Trust)**
	1. I trust my body to tell me when to eat.

	2. I trust my body to tell me what to eat.
	3. I trust my body to tell me how much to eat.
	4. I rely on my hunger signals to tell me when to eat.
	5. I rely on my fullness (satiety) signals to tell me when to stop eating.
	6. I trust my body when to stop eating.
Yes/No	**Section 4. Body—Food Choice Congruence**
	1. Most of the time, I desire to eat nutritious foods.
	2. I mostly eat foods that make my body perform efficiently (well).
	3. I mostly eat foods that give my body energy and stamina.

Scoring

Sections 1-2: Each "yes" statement indicates an area that likely needs some work.

Section 3-4: Each "no" statement indicates an area that likely need some work.

Sources

[1]. Tylka, Tracy L. (2006). Development and psychometric evaluation of a measure of intuitive eating. Journal of Counseling Psychology 53(2), Apr:226--240.

[2] Tylka, T.L. (2013). A psychometric evaluation of the Intuitive Eating Scale with college men. Journal of Counseling Psychology, Jan;60(1):137--53.

[3] Tribole E. & Resch E. (2012). Intuitive Eating (3rd ed). St.Martin's Press, NY:NY.

Looking at the answers to your assessment, what areas of your relationship with food and body are flourishing?

What areas are you struggling with?

What ideas do you have for why you struggle in these areas? What ideas do you have for making improvements here?

Write a prayer below asking God to transform your mind in these areas. Write down anything else He's revealing to you.

📽 Finding a Why that's Deeper than Weight

"We have this hope as an anchor for the soul, firm and steadfast. It enters the inner sanctuary behind the curtain..." Hebrews 6:19

After watching the video, "Finding a Why that's Deeper than Weight," take time to answer these questions:

What numbers / things / people have you been putting your hope in?

When these things fail you, how are you affected? How does this kind of failure affect how you feel about and relate to God?

What good thing are you really after? What have you believed weight loss, body change, etc will give you?

Pause and ponder the possibility of having these good things without becoming enslaved to the scale god, the food tracking god, or the food label god...

Describe what life would be like, what would you be able to do differently, if you felt you had what you were after.

"And we all, who with unveiled faces contemplate the Lord's glory, are being transformed into his image with ever-increasing glory, which comes from the Lord, who is the Spirit." 2 Corinthians 3:18

Move Free

 ## How Exercise Can Support Your Season

"For everything there is a season, and a time for every purpose under heaven"
Ecclesiastes 3:1

After watching the video, "How Exercise Can Support Your Season," complete the assessment and take time to answer the following questions:

Joyful Movement Self-Assessment

Agree / Disagree	Section 1: Permission to Allow Fitness to Fit You
	1. A workout only counts for me if I'm sore, sweaty, or burning calories.
	2. If I know I need to rest my body, I exercise anyways.
	3. I get mad at myself for not spending time exercising, no matter the life circumstance.
	4. Walking, stretching, and breathing do not count as exercise.
	5. I follow plans that dictate how much and when to exercise without taking into consideration my enjoyment level or level of meaning for me.
	6. I feel a sense of guilt around exercise.
Agree / Disagree	Section 2. Learning Intuitive Movement Cues
	1. I exercise more when I want to change my body size.
	2. I workout to earn or to payoff food.
	3. I don't typically address body cues like lethargy, stiff joints, insomnia, breathlessness, and impaired physical ability in daily life with intentional movement care.
	4. I don't typically address body cues like stiff and sore muscles, heavy limbs, overuse injuries, achy joints, reduced energy, and illness with appropriate rest and recovery.

Agree / Disagree	Section 3: Movement Choice Congruence
	5. I'm not sure if I have moved "enough" or what movement satisfaction feels like.
	Section 3: Movement Choice Congruence
	1. I believe moving during the day counts towards my body's movement needs.
	2. I feel confident to plan and commit to a supplementary movement plan that fits my season of life. I know where to seek help when needed.
	3. As a whole, I move in a balanced way to take care of all parts of my body: cardio for heart and lungs, resistance for bones and muscles, stretching and mobility work for connective tissue.
	4. For the most part, I move in a way that supports my wellbeing and life goals as I feel called by God.

Scoring

Sections 1-2: Each "agree" statement indicates an area that likely needs some work.

Section 3: Each "disagree" statement indicates an area that likely need some work.

What is your season of life right now?

Does your season of life have an end date?

Ex: My season of life is being a mom of a one-year-old and a kindergartener, a fitness instructor and personal trainer. My current timeline is defined by the end of the school year.

Fitness outcomes are a product of habits, which flow from identity. Decide **who** you are in Christ before you get into the **why** and **how** of movement.

Now that you have defined your season, prayerfully answer the following:
God, the person you are forming me into in this season of _____ is to be
_____. This is my Joy Goal.

Ex: God, the person you are forming me into during this season of <u>motherhood</u> is to be <u>humble</u>.

A few other examples of identity formation could be:
- Kind
- Disciplined
- Patient

Now you may decide how fitness supports the person you already are in the Lord, starting with His grace instead of your own effort. You simply get to step into His life and let the joy flow naturally!

For example, if you want to focus on being **kind** this season, you may want to lean into the intuitive side of movement and discover what fits your body best. If you want to focus on being **disciplined**, think of what a disciplined person would do for fitness, and follow through accordingly in God's strength. If you want to become more **patient** in the Lord, you might choose a path of endurance with results that pay off later, like a long run or holding passive poses in yoga.

Write a prayer to ask God any other details of how He wants to form you into His image during this season:

Your Fitness Motivator Quiz

Take the Motivator Quiz to give you more guidance about what kind of exercise can support your season of life. Highlight yours, watch your corresponding video, and continue with the questions below. Please reference the motivator guide in Appendix A for a summary of traits and exercise recommendations.

After each of the multiple-choice questions, there is a number in parenthesis. Pick the one that most fits you right now. Keep a tally of those numbers to get your score.

1) Which fitness headline appeals to me most?

   a) "Best Circuit Workout: Think You Can Handle It?" (4)

   b) "Strong and Sexy" (1)

   c) "Energy Blast" (3)

   d) "Instant Calm" (2)

   e) "Nourish Your Body" (5)

2) At the beginning of the day, I struggle with:

   a) Choosing which awesome thing I want to do (4)

   b) My mile-long to-do list (3)

   c) My reflection in the mirror (1)

   d) Stress (2)

   e) Thinking about how to prevent injury (5)

3) I choose a workout based on:

   a) The epic factor: if I can learn a new skill or explore new territory, I'm in. (4)

   b) A science-backed plan proven to boost immunity and banish disease. (5)

   c) How many calories does it burn? Will it fix my trouble zones? (1)

   d) How peaceful I will feel. (2)

   e) How efficient it will be: What workout has the most multitasking moves in 20 minutes?

      (3)

4) My exercise tipping point is:

a) Seeing pictures of myself (1)

b) Needing to let off some steam (2)

c) Overhearing a friend talk about how awesome their group workout is (4)

d) Feeling guilty over skipping a planned workout (3)

e) Getting less-than-ideal lab results back from the doctor (5)

5) I avoid exercise because:

a) It's too painful. (5)

b) There are too many people at the gym and I'm not fit enough yet. (1)

c) The last plan was too rigid. (2)

d) It's boring and not challenging enough by myself. (4)

e) I'm taking care of everyone else and don't have time. (3)

6) Deep down, I want to:

a) Have energy to focus on what's important. (3)

b) Shift my focus from my body to other parts of my life. (1)

c) Be a ninja of tranquility with a balanced, strong interior that isn't shaken by external

circumstances. (2)

d) Be a positive example for the next generation. (5)

e) Know I am capable, powerful, and connected with others. (4)

7) I like this feeling after a workout:

a) Pumped up, walking tall (1)

b) Energized, with more to give (3)

c) Sweaty high fives (4)

d) Settled and put together (2)

e) To hear, "Great job today!" (5)

8) My usual long-term fitness goal is motivated by:

a) Training for a race, competition, or other challenge (4)

b) A special event, like a beach trip, reunion, or wedding (1)

c) What long-term goal? (2)

d) Avoiding genetic diseases (5)

e) A workout plan that fits into my already determined schedule (3)

9) What inspires me to move:

a) Finding a workout that helps me look like the fitness instructor or superhero on screen

(1)

b) New challenges and friendly competition (4)

c) Escaping, whether that's through meditation, music, or getting outside (2)

d) Having a results-based plan with no unnecessary downtime (3)

e) A health professional keeping me accountable (5)

10) This distracts me, and I think a workout can help!

a) Aches and pains are annoying, but not something I have time to address. (3)

b) I'm tired of feeling unhealthy, whether that's from extra weight, fatigue, pain, or other

illness. (5)

c) Overstimulation and overwork. (2)

d) I can't wait to unlock my hidden potential and be the best I was created to be. (4)

e) Tight-fitting clothes makes me unable to focus on the rest of my life. (1)

SCORING:

10-17: Looker (page 23)

18-25: Freebird (page 24)

26-34: Hero (page 25)

35-42: Warrior (page 26)

43-50: Keeper (page 27)

Find your motivator, watch your video, and head to the corresponding questions in the following section.

Looker

Colossians 3:12: "Put on then, as God's chosen ones, holy and beloved, compassionate hearts, kindness, humility, meekness, and patience."

Draw an outline of yourself on a piece of paper. Look in a full-length mirror, and write on the piece of paper where you are unhappy with your body and where you got that idea using the three F's:
   a) Family
   b) Friends
   c) Facebook (general social media)

How has your family said is an acceptable way to look? What did a friend say to you in the past? How does Facebook play a role in the comparison trap?

Comparison is the thief of joy, but gratitude is the giver of joy. Lay down with palms open, and starting from your toes, give thanks to God for each part of your body, working up to your head. Stop on the parts of your body you are unhappy with and ask God how He sees you. Remember, He doesn't even look on external appearances, but at your heart. Receive His sight and be loved.

After this exercise, using the same picture you drew above, write with a marker the truth the Lord revealed to you from the previous exercise over the top of any negative comments you might have written down.

Turn the paper over and write Colossians 3:12 from above at the top.

Instead of taking away from yourself with exercise by worrying about how many calories you're burning or fat you're melting off, ask Jesus to forgive the old ways of striving and shame, to take away the heart heaviness. Then, put on His covering of compassion, kindness, humility, meekness, and patience as a royal robe. Start with thanking God that you are chosen and beloved. Write down how being loved frees you up for joyful movement. Refer to Appendix A for concrete ideas.

You did it! Go ahead and jump down to "Going Forward" on page 28.

Freebird

"Or do you not know that your body is a temple of the Holy Spirit within you, whom you have from God?" 1 Corinthians 6:19

What is your source of stress right now? Name everything that comes to mind:

Feel it: get quiet, close your eyes, and pinpoint the strongest sensation in your body. Often, our physical symptoms are connected to emotions. Describe the sensation (ex: heart racing, lower back aching, head throbbing):

Whatever you are dwelling on that is not of the Lord, step away and back into His dwelling place, which is the temple of your body. Be in your body, with Him! Jesus hiked up mountains to get away with God. Consider how you can use movement to help relieve your source of stress. If you're feeling rushed, a slow and creative flow might be what you need. If your current environment feels chaotic, moving yourself to a new location might be helpful. When in doubt, walking outdoors or doing some type of repetitive cardio always helps to relieve stress.

Write down some ideas that have helped you in the past, and how you can use movement as a tool for freedom in times of stress:

At the beginning of your chosen movement, take a deep inhale, putting your hands around your ribcage and expanding your sides, letting the breath extend down past your belly button, and exhale the source of stress, making room for the Lord to fill up His temple. On your inhale, invite His joy to push out the stress. Continue this practice, praying "Jesus" on the inhale, and "sets me free" on the exhale during your exercise until you feel free and full of His joy!

Refer to Appendix A for more specific encouragement for the Freebird.

Go ahead and jump down to "Going Forward" on page 28.

Hero

"Therefore, if anyone cleanses himself from what is dishonorable, he will be a vessel for honorable use, set apart as holy, useful to the master of the house, ready for every good work." 2 Timothy 2:21

You want to be ready for every good work, and useful to the master of the house. You don't need to do everything, but as 1 Corinthians 15:58 says, "Give yourself fully to the work of the Lord." Let everything else go. What do you need to let go of? This is part of "cleaning yourself from what is dishonorable," throwing off what is not yours to own, and using exercise as a gift to fill you up for His good works.

Write down a time of day you feel least energized. How could movement help?

Are there times you don't allow yourself to exercise? Why?

What workouts wear you out for the work God has called you to in this season? Consider cutting them out of your routine or modifying them.

Which movements energize you? Keep these routines ready to go. Head to Appendix A for more ideas.

Go ahead and jump down to "Going Forward" on page 28.

Warrior

"Instead, speaking the truth in love, we will grow to become in every respect the mature body of him who is the head, that is, Christ. From him the whole body, joined and held together by every supporting ligament, grows and builds itself up in love, as each part does its work." Ephesians 4:15-16

Do you like working out with people, or would you rather compete against yourself in a workout? If you enjoy being in solitude, what fires you up? If with people, with whom and in what context?

What kinds of movement push you beyond your normal limits and make you feel alive?

How can opening your eyes to see Jesus beside you challenge you in your next workout?

Where do you feel weak in your fitness journey, and who in your life is strong in this area? How can you connect with them as the body of Christ?

Where do you feel strong in fitness, and how can you serve someone else who feels weak in this area?

Go ahead and jump down to "Going Forward" on page 28.

Keeper

"So we make it our goal to please him, whether we are at home in the body or away from it." 2 Corinthians 5:9, NIV

If you could rate your health on a scale of 1-5, one being sick and struggling, and 5 being thriving and well, where would you be?

What kind of scales do you think the Lord uses to rate you (see Proverbs 16:11, James 2:23)?

Write down how Jesus' unconditional love makes you feel, and how that frees you from exercise either giving you value or devaluing you.

What you listen for, you will hear. Who do you listen to most when it comes to your fitness? Your body? Online or personal trainers? Your own conscience? The Holy Spirit? What are you listening for, and hoping to hear?

How can the Lord use our body as a way to communicate (see Psalm 143:6, Matthew 5:6, Galatians 2:2), and how can you pause and listen to Him through your own body today? You may reference Appendix A for more ideas on the Keeper.

Going Forward

Now that you have your Joy Goal and Motivator in mind, answer the following about your season right now:

How can targeted exercise help? '

What kind of exercise could hurt?

What is the effect of not exercising?

Before moving, commit to pray a simple prayer based on your Motivator to keep your efforts rooted in grace:

Suggestions:
Looker: "In Christ"
Freebird: "With the Lord"
Hero: "Filled with His presence"
Warrior: "With my brothers and sisters in Christ"
Keeper: "All for the Lord"

By Grace

Lord, thank you for teaching me...

WEEK OF: _____

Menu Sketch

Use the space below to brainstorm meal and snack ideas for the week and to create a grocery list. Don't worry about what day you will eat each item. Your appetite and schedule could change throughout the week. Taco Tuesday just might turn into Taco Monday, etc. If you need help, consult the other members of your household. Kids especially love to add their two cents.

Dinner Ideas   **GROCERY LIST**

1.

2.

3.

4.

5.

6.

Lunch Ideas

1.

2.

3.

Breakfast Ideas

1.

2.

3.

Snacks & Fun Foods

1.

2.

3.

WEEK OF: _____

Exercise Ideas

Use the space below to jot down ways you would like to exercise this week. If it helps you with logistics, fill in the week below with your plans. Make sure to schedule same muscle group strength sessions on non-consecutive days and include an active rest day. Use the FITT recommendations provided in the Introduction on page 6 to guide you, but feel free to change it up based on your body and day's needs.

What I already enjoy
1.
2.
3.
4.
5.

Cardio Ideas (3-5x/week)
1.
2.
3.
4.
5.

Strength Ideas (2-3x/week)
1.
2.
3.

Stretch/Mobility Ideas (2-7x/week)
1.
2.
3.

	Sun	Mon	Tues	Wed	Thurs	Fri	Sat
What I'm Already Doing							
How I can add strength							
How I can add cardio							
How I can add mobility							

DATE: _____

Romans 12:2

"Do not be conformed to this world, but be transformed by the renewal of your mind, that by testing you may discern what is the will of God, what is good and acceptable and perfect."

Today, I'm grateful for

Time	Hunger*	What I ate	Fullness*	Satisfaction*	Notes

Fitness Felt Need*	Time	Workout	Before	After	Notes

Rate hunger, fullness and satisfaction on scale of 1-10. Reference hunger/fullness scale and fitness felt needs on pages 5-6.

Other self-care I engaged in:

Prayer:

DATE: _____

Ephesians 2:8-9

"For by grace you have been saved through faith. And this is not your own doing; it is the gift of God, not a result of works, so that no one may boast."

Today, I'm grateful for

Time	Hunger*	What I ate	Fullness*	Satisfaction*	Notes

Fitness Felt Need*	Time	Workout	Before	After	Notes

Rate hunger, fullness and satisfaction on scale of 1-10. Reference hunger/fullness scale and fitness felt needs on pages 5-6.

Other self-care I engaged in:

Prayer:

DATE: _____

Hebrews 6:19

"We have this hope as an anchor for the soul, firm and steadfast. It enters the inner sanctuary behind the curtain…"

Today, I'm grateful for

Time	Hunger*	What I ate	Fullness*	Satisfaction*	Notes

Fitness Felt Need	Time	Workout	Before	After	Notes

Rate hunger, fullness and satisfaction on scale of 1-10. Reference hunger/fullness scale and fitness felt needs on pages 5-6.

Other self-care I engaged in:

Prayer:

STRENGTH EXERCISE		Date	Date	Date	Date	Date	Notes
	Weight						
	Reps						
	Sets						
	RPE						
	Weight						
	Reps						
	Sets						
	RPE						
	Weight						
	Reps						
	Sets						
	RPE						
	Weight						
	Reps						
	Sets						
	RPE						
	Weight						
	Reps						
	Sets						
	RPE						
	Weight						
	Reps						
	Sets						
	RPE						
CARDIO EXERCISE		Date	Date	Date	Date	Date	Date
	Time						
	Distance						
	Intensity*						
	Time						
	Distance						
	Intensity*						

RPE: 1-10 Rate of Perceived Exertion*Intensity: L/M/V Light/Moderate/Vigorous or HR

Week Two

Eat Well

📹 Differentiating Health and Weight

"Nevertheless, I will bring health and healing to it; I will heal my people and will let them enjoy abundant peace and security." Jeremiah 33:6 (NIV)

After watching the video, "Differentiating Health and Weight," take time to answer the questions below:

When you think about health, does weight immediately come to mind? If so, why do you think that is? Can you think of a definition of health that doesn't include weight?

List the different areas of your life where you want to experience health (mental, relational, emotional, physical, etc). Now describe what health would look and feel like in each category.

What are some healthy behaviors/habits that you already practice?

We will talk about habit change with the Holy Spirit later and throughout this course, but to start, what are some immediate healthy behaviors you hope to implement? List ones that seem more doable/important first. These don't have to be food/exercise related, they could address spiritual, emotional or relational health too, all of which are equally as important as physical health.

🎥 Returning to Your Body's Preferred Rhythm for Eating

"'For you created my inmost being; you knit me together in my mother's womb. I praise you because I am fearfully and wonderfully made; your works are wonderful, I know that full well." Psalm 139:13-14 (NIV)

After watching the video, "Returning to Your Body's Preferred Rhythm for Eating," take time to answer the questions below:

Pick at least one day this week and write down when you ate and what you ate. If you like, you can use the food journal provided at the beginning of each week.

Note: When are you going too long without eating? You can figure this out by noting when you became overly hungry, felt out of control when eating your next meal, or when you simply went longer than 5 hours without eating.

Use the chart below to make a new schedule of eating for a typical weekday and another one for a typical weekend day. Aim to eat within 1 hour of waking and at least every 3-4 hours afterwards throughout the day (or before, if you're hungry earlier).

Note: this is not a strict schedule, it's just to get you brainstorming about ways to fit in adequate nourishment throughout your day. Also, you do not have to eat 6 meals/snacks a day if this doesn't fit with your lifestyle.

Meal	Weekday Time | Food Examples	Weekend Time | Food Examples
Breakfast		
Morning Snack		
Lunch		
Afternoon snack		
Dinner		
Evening snack		

Practically, what will you need to do to implement this schedule (pack snacks the night before, stock your fridge at work, prep breakfast, etc.)?

Our goal is to eat enough to be full and satisfied until the next meal/snack. Are there areas in your day where you feel you may need to add more food to a meal or snack or where you need to add more satisfying (pleasurable) foods?

Move Free

📽 Baseline Testing: Where Are You?

"But the LORD God called to the man and said to him, 'Where are you?'" Genesis 3:9

After watching the video, "Baseline Testing: Where Are You," complete your fitness test according to the video instructions. If this test does not apply to what you would like to assess for your own body, create your own assessment here that you can duplicate after the 12 weeks (photos, set of journal questions, quizzing family members about your attitude before and after the course, etc):

Fitness Test

Date						
Cardio Rockport 1 mile test* Resting HR						
Finish HR						
Finish time						
Mobility* Supine Hamstring Stretch						
Behind the head reach						
Balance Single leg stand						
Strength Wall sit						
Push-ups						
Plank hold						

*Rockport Walk Test: After warming up, walk as fast as possible for one mile. Record heart rate in beats per minute with a heart rate monitor or manually, and time of completion. Head here to plug in results: https://exrx.net/calculators/rockport

Create Your Fitness Plan

"Do not despise these small beginnings, for the LORD rejoices to see the work begin…" Zechariah 4:10 (NLT)

Write down your exercise intention:

Each week, I will move [in this way] on [these days] at [this time] in [this place] because God is forming me into being [identity word] in this season of [name your season.]*

Example: Each week, I will move [on a walk with my neighbor] on [MWF] at [4:30pm] in [our neighborhood] because God is forming me into being [faithful] in this season of [transition.]

"For those whom he foreknew he also predestined to be conformed to the image of his Son, in order that he might be the firstborn among many brothers." Romans 8:29

In John 21:15, Jesus tells Simon Peter to take care of the weakest members first. When we care for the members of our body in a grateful relationship, we practice caring for members of the body of Christ. How can you protect and take care of your body in this season?

"For the moment all discipline seems painful rather than pleasant, but later it yields the peaceful fruit of righteousness to those who have been trained by it." Hebrews 12:11

What exercise do you need to do?

What would you like to do for exercise? Refer to your motivator exercise video or Appendix A for ideas of how to implement this regularly.

Working backwards from your Joy Goal SMART plan, write down an incremental plan for yourself, as modeled in the video.

Goal day accomplishment:

Working backwards from your goal day, outline your plan below:

Today, I will:

Using the FITT Guide below, and the Exercise Ideas page at the end of this week's content, set your weekly exercise intentions. Refer to the Fitness Felt Needs chart on page 6 for additional help.

	Frequency	Intensity	Time	Type
Strength	2-3 / week	Perform each set until muscle fatigue	2-3 sets of 4-15 repetitions for each major muscle group	Include all major muscle groups: legs, chest, back, biceps, triceps, shoulders, core
Cardio	3-5 / week	Exert 60-90% effort	20-60 minutes / session	Include all major muscle groups
Mobility	2-7 / week	Stretch to full range of motion without pain	15-30 seconds / stretch	Include all major muscle groups

By Grace

Lord, thank you for teaching me...

WEEK OF: _____

Menu Sketch

Use the space below to brainstorm meal and snack ideas for the week and to create a grocery list. Don't worry about what day you will eat each item. Your appetite and schedule could change throughout the week. Taco Tuesday just might turn into Taco Monday, etc. If you need help, consult the other members of your household. Kids especially love to add their two cents.

Dinner Ideas   **GROCERY LIST**

1.

2.

3.

4.

5.

6.

Lunch Ideas

1.

2.

3.

Breakfast Ideas

1.

2.

3.

Snacks & Fun Foods

1.

2.

3.

WEEK OF: _____

Exercise Ideas

Use the space below to jot down ways you would like to exercise this week. If it helps you with logistics, fill in the week below with your plans. Make sure to schedule same muscle group strength sessions on non-consecutive days and include an active rest day. Use the FITT recommendations provided in the Introduction on page 6 to guide you, but feel free to change it up based on your body and day's needs.

What I already enjoy
1.
2.
3.
4.
5.

Cardio Ideas (3-5x/week)
1.
2.
3.
4.
5.

Strength Ideas (2-3x/week)
1.
2.
3.

Stretch/Mobility Ideas (2-7x/week)
1.
2.
3.

	Sun	Mon	Tues	Wed	Thurs	Fri	Sat
What I'm Already Doing							
How I can add strength							
How I can add cardio							
How I can add mobility							

DATE: _____

Jeremiah 33:6

"'Nevertheless, I will bring health and healing to it; I will heal my people and will let them enjoy abundant peace and security."

Today, I'm grateful for

Time	Hunger*	What I ate	Fullness*	Satisfaction*	Notes

Fitness Felt Need*	Time	Workout	Before	After	Notes

Rate hunger, fullness and satisfaction on scale of 1-10. Reference hunger/fullness scale and fitness felt needs on pages 5-6.

Other self-care I engaged in:

Prayer:

DATE: _____

Zachariah 4:10

"Do not despise these small beginnings, for the LORD rejoices to see the work begin..."

Today, I'm grateful for

Time	Hunger*	What I ate	Fullness*	Satisfaction*	Notes

Fitness Felt Need*	Time	Workout	Before	After	Notes

Rate hunger, fullness and satisfaction on scale of 1-10. Reference hunger/fullness scale and fitness felt needs on pages 5-6.

Other self-care I engaged in:

Prayer:

DATE: _____

Psalm 139:14

"I praise you, for I am fearfully and wonderfully made. Wonderful are your works; my soul knows it very well."

Today, I'm grateful for

Time	Hunger*	What I ate	Fullness*	Satisfaction*	Notes

Fitness Felt Need	Time	Workout	Before	After	Notes

Rate hunger, fullness and satisfaction on scale of 1-10. Reference hunger/fullness scale and fitness felt needs on pages 5-6.

Other self-care I engaged in:

Prayer:

STRENGTH EXERCISE		Date	Date	Date	Date	Date	Notes
	Weight						
	Reps						
	Sets						
	RPE						
	Weight						
	Reps						
	Sets						
	RPE						
	Weight						
	Reps						
	Sets						
	RPE						
	Weight						
	Reps						
	Sets						
	RPE						
	Weight						
	Reps						
	Sets						
	RPE						
	Weight						
	Reps						
	Sets						
	RPE						
CARDIO EXERCISE		Date	Date	Date	Date	Date	Notes
	Time						
	Distance						
	Intensity*						
	Time						
	Distance						
	Intensity*						

RPE: 1-10 Rate of Perceived Exertion*Intensity: L/M/V Light/Moderate/Vigorous or HR

Week Three

Eat Well

All Foods Fit, Making Peace with Fear Foods

"They forbid people to marry and order them to abstain from certain foods, which God created to be received with thanksgiving by those who believe and who know the truth. For everything God created is good, and nothing is to be rejected if it is received with thanksgiving, because it is consecrated by the word of God and prayer." 1 Timothy 2: 3-5

After watching the video, "All Foods Fit, Making Peace with Fear Foods," take time to answer the questions below:

What foods have you typically viewed as good or safe?

What foods have you typically seen as bad or unsafe?

Did you always believe those foods were bad? How did you come to view them that way?

What foods do you feel out of control around? Which ones do you really love eating? List them from least to most worrisome below.

Pick one food from the top of the list that you want to make peace with this week. Plan to eat this food every day with a regular meal or snack, preferably in a safe, calm environment with family/friends. As mentioned in the video, we will eat this food (same brand, same flavor) until it is no longer fear provoking or we no longer crave it.

Below, write the food, when you will eat it, where or with whom and how you will care for yourself afterward.

Take it one step further, what positive qualities does this food have (think nutrition, flavor, enjoyment, associations, etc)? Another way to think of this: What good things is this food providing for your body?

Move Free

📹 Set up Support, Accountability, and Celebrate

"Therefore, since we are surrounded by so great a cloud of witnesses, let us also lay aside every weight, and sin which clings so closely, and let us run with endurance the race that is set before us," Hebrews 12:1

After watching the video, "Set up Support, Accountability, and Celebrate," take time to answer the following questions:

How can you share your desires for exercise with those you live with?

Who is one encouraging person that you can share your season, struggle, and plan with? Write his or her name and what they will hold you accountable for:

Here's what each motivator might say as a prayer of thanksgiving in the moment and to celebrate a big Joy Goal milestone:

	Give thanks	Milestone celebration
Looker	"You see me"	Buy yourself new workout clothes
Freebird	"You're with me"	Splurge on a new class
Hero	"You're enough"	Get a massage
Warrior	"Your love doesn't quit"	Go out with friends for smoothies
Keeper	"You approve"	Invest in a course, planner, or fitness app

How can you give thanks in the moment?

How will you celebrate in participation with your God who already celebrates you (Zephaniah 3:17)...

At the end of a fun workout:

At the end of each week:

At the end of your season:

By Grace

Lord, thank you for teaching me...

WEEK OF: _____

Menu Sketch

Use the space below to brainstorm meal and snack ideas for the week and to create a grocery list. Don't worry about what day you will eat each item. Your appetite and schedule could change throughout the week. Taco Tuesday just might turn into Taco Monday, etc. If you need help, consult the other members of your household. Kids especially love to add their two cents.

Dinner Ideas   **GROCERY LIST**

1.

2.

3.

4.

5.

6.

Lunch Ideas

1.

2.

3.

Breakfast Ideas

1.

2.

3.

Snacks & Fun Foods

1.

2.

3.

Exercise Ideas

Use the space below to jot down ways you would like to exercise this week. If it helps you with logistics, fill in the week below with your plans. Make sure to schedule same muscle group strength sessions on non-consecutive days and include an active rest day. Use the FITT recommendations provided in the Introduction on page 6 to guide you, but feel free to change it up based on your body and day's needs.

What I already enjoy

1.

2.

3.

4.

5.

Cardio Ideas (3-5x/week)

1.

2.

3.

4.

5.

Strength Ideas (2-3x/week)

1.

2.

3.

Stretch/Mobility Ideas (2-7x/week)

1.

2.

3.

	Sun	Mon	Tues	Wed	Thurs	Fri	Sat
What I'm Already Doing							
How I can add strength							
How I can add cardio							
How I can add mobility							

DATE: _____

1 Timothy 2: 4-5

"For everything God created is good, and nothing is to be rejected if it is received with thanksgiving, because it is consecrated by the word of God and prayer."

Today, I'm grateful for

Time	Hunger*	What I ate	Fullness*	Satisfaction*	Notes

Fitness Felt Need*	Time	Workout	Before	After	Notes

Rate hunger, fullness and satisfaction on scale of 1-10. Reference hunger/fullness scale and fitness felt needs on pages 5-6.

Other self-care I engaged in:

Prayer:

DATE: _____

Hebrews 12:1

"Therefore, since we are surrounded by so great a cloud of witnesses, let us also lay aside every weight, and sin which clings so closely, and let us run with endurance the race that is set before us"

Today, I'm grateful for

Time	Hunger*	What I ate	Fullness*	Satisfaction*	Notes

Fitness Felt Need*	Time	Workout	Before	After	Notes

Rate hunger, fullness and satisfaction on scale of 1-10. Reference hunger/fullness scale and fitness felt needs on pages 5-6.

Other self-care I engaged in:

Prayer:

DATE: _____

Zephaniah 3:17

" The LORD your God is in your midst, a mighty one who will save; he will rejoice over you with gladness; he will quiet you by his love; he will exult over you with loud singing."

Today, I'm grateful for

Time	Hunger*	What I ate	Fullness*	Satisfaction*	Notes

Fitness Felt Need	Time	Workout	Before	After	Notes

Rate hunger, fullness and satisfaction on scale of 1-10. Reference hunger/fullness scale and fitness felt needs on pages 5-6.

Other self-care I engaged in:

Prayer:

Week Three

STRENGTH EXERCISE		Date	Date	Date	Date	Date	Notes
	Weight						
	Reps						
	Sets						
	RPE						
	Weight						
	Reps						
	Sets						
	RPE						
	Weight						
	Reps						
	Sets						
	RPE						
	Weight						
	Reps						
	Sets						
	RPE						
	Weight						
	Reps						
	Sets						
	RPE						
	Weight						
	Reps						
	Sets						
	RPE						
CARDIO EXERCISE		Date	Date	Date	Date	Date	Date
	Time						
	Distance						
	Intensity*						
	Time						
	Distance						
	Intensity*						

RPE: 1-10 Rate of Perceived Exertion*Intensity: L/M/V Light/Moderate/Vigorous or HR

Week Four

Eat Well

🎥 Discerning Hunger and Fullness

"For no one ever hated his own flesh, but nourishes and cherishes it, just as Christ does the church..." Ephesians 5:29

After watching the video, "Discerning Hunger and Fullness," take time to answer the questions below:

Are you consistently eating at regular intervals throughout the day? If not, how can you tweak your day to stay nourished?

Are you restricting amounts or types of food at this time? Are you still working through fear foods? If so, please continue to do this one food at a time until foods no longer feel scary. List your plan for trialing foods below.

Use the journal pages at the beginning of each week to track intake for at least three days in a row and rate hunger, fullness, and satisfaction. Remember there is no right or wrong here, just information to consider and learn from.

What patterns arose as you tracked? What did you notice helped you stay full for longer? Did satisfaction make a difference? When were times you were too hungry? What are some tactics you can put into practice to help you stay better fueled?

Move Free

📽 All or Nothing Mindset

"So, my dear brothers and sisters, be strong and immovable. Always work enthusiastically for the Lord, for you know that nothing you do for the Lord is ever useless." 1 Corinthians 15:58

After watching the video, "All or Nothing Mindset," take time to answer the questions below:

When and how does the "all or nothing" mindset discourage you on your fitness journey? How do you react? How would you like to respond?

Would you rather commit to a certain program, or to God's path? How can you discern the difference between the two?

When do you feel you get off track with the kind of exercise you've been wanting to do? Name all the variables: work deadlines, childcare, unpredictable schedule, etc. Ask our creative God to open your heart to all of His ways (see Psalm 78:13).

Submit your exercise plan from Week Two to the Lord in prayer. What do you think He wants to grow in you through exercise (see Galatians 5)?

Write down your levels from 1 to 5, naming the corresponding circumstance and exercise that fits the occasion.

Example:
Level 1: All the kids are sick—do 5 minutes of yoga before crawling in bed at night

Level 5: Everything is going as planned—Hit the gym for 1 hour before everyone wakes up

Level 1

Level 2

Level 3

Level 4

Level 5

Make creating a new habit seamless and pain-free. How could you make moving a part of your natural rhythms and habitat?

By Grace

Lord, thank you for teaching me...

WEEK OF: _____

Menu Sketch

Use the space below to brainstorm meal and snack ideas for the week and to create a grocery list. Don't worry about what day you will eat each item. Your appetite and schedule could change throughout the week. Taco Tuesday just might turn into Taco Monday, etc. If you need help, consult the other members of your household. Kids especially love to add their two cents.

Dinner Ideas   **GROCERY LIST**

1.

2.

3.

4.

5.

6.

Lunch Ideas

1.

2.

3.

Breakfast Ideas

1.

2.

3.

Snacks & Fun Foods

1.

2.

3.

WEEK OF: _____

Exercise Ideas

Use the space below to jot down ways you would like to exercise this week. If it helps you with logistics, fill in the week below with your plans. Make sure to schedule same muscle group strength sessions on non-consecutive days and include an active rest day. Use the FITT recommendations provided in the Introduction on page 6 to guide you, but feel free to change it up based on your body and day's needs.

What I already enjoy

1.

2.

3.

4.

5.

Cardio Ideas (3-5x/week)

1.

2.

3.

4.

5.

Strength Ideas (2-3x/week)

1.

2.

3.

Stretch/Mobility Ideas (2-7x/week)

1.

2.

3.

	Sun	Mon	Tues	Wed	Thurs	Fri	Sat
What I'm Already Doing							
How I can add strength							
How I can add cardio							
How I can add mobility							

DATE: _____

Ephesians 5:29

"For no one ever hated his own flesh, but nourishes and cherishes it, just as Christ does the church"

Today, I'm grateful for

Time	Hunger*	What I ate	Fullness*	Satisfaction*	Notes

Fitness Felt Need*	Time	Workout	Before	After	Notes

Rate hunger, fullness and satisfaction on scale of 1-10. Reference hunger/fullness scale and fitness felt needs on page 5-6

Other self-care I engaged in:

Prayer:

DATE: _____

1st Corinthians 15:58

"So, my dear brothers and sisters, be strong and immovable. Always work enthusiastically for the Lord, for you know that nothing you do for the Lord is ever useless."

Today, I'm grateful for

Time	Hunger*	What I ate	Fullness*	Satisfaction*	Notes

Fitness Felt Need*	Time	Workout	Before	After	Notes

Rate hunger, fullness and satisfaction on scale of 1-10. Reference hunger/fullness scale and fitness felt needs on pages 5-6.

Other self-care I engaged in:

Prayer:

DATE: _____

Galatians 5: 22-23

"But the fruit of the Spirit is love, joy, peace, forbearance, kindness, goodness, faithfulness, gentleness, and self-control."

Today, I'm grateful for

Time	Hunger*	What I ate	Fullness*	Satisfaction*	Notes

Fitness Felt Need	Time	Workout	Before	After	Notes

Rate hunger, fullness and satisfaction on scale of 1-10. Reference hunger/fullness scale and fitness felt needs on pages 5-6.

Other self-care I engaged in:

Prayer:

Week Four

STRENGTH EXERCISE		Date	Date	Date	Date	Date	Notes
	Weight						
	Reps						
	Sets						
	RPE						
	Weight						
	Reps						
	Sets						
	RPE						
	Weight						
	Reps						
	Sets						
	RPE						
	Weight						
	Reps						
	Sets						
	RPE						
	Weight						
	Reps						
	Sets						
	RPE						
	Weight						
	Reps						
	Sets						
	RPE						
CARDIO EXERCISE		Date	Date	Date	Date	Date	Notes
	Time						
	Distance						
	Intensity*						
	Time						
	Distance						
	Intensity*						

RPE: 1-10 Rate of Perceived Exertion*Intensity: L/M/V Light/Moderate/Vigorous or HR

74

MONTH OF:_____

Joyful Health at a Glance

SUN	MON	TUES	WED	THURS	FRI	SAT

Week Five

Eat Well

📹 Considering Nutritional Balance

"Do not forsake wisdom, and she will protect you; love her, and she will watch over you. The beginning of wisdom is this: Get wisdom. Though it costs all you have, get understanding." Proverbs 4:6-7

After watching the video, "Considering Nutritional Balance," take time to answer the questions below:

Use the example plate to fill the blank plates below with sample meals. These should be meals you have regularly or enjoy eating. After watching the video, make sure to add balance where it's needed. For example, if you usually eat spaghetti with sauce and broccoli and you are looking to add some protein, fun and fat, consider making it with hamburger or lentils, and adding a cheese and/or a dessert, etc.

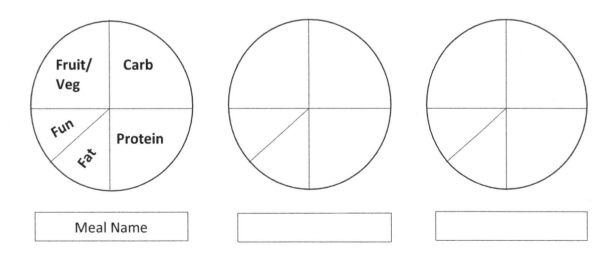

List a few more balanced menu ideas for each meal below.

Breakfast   Lunch   Dinner

List a few snack ideas below. Remember snacks can be mini meals or they can be fun foods. Our aim is to have at least two of the macronutrient groups in each snack (carbs, fat, and protein).

Move Free

Consistency Over Calorie Burn

"And let us not grow weary of doing good, for in due season we will reap, if we do not give up." Galatians 6:9

After watching the video, "Consistency over Calorie Burn," take time to answer the questions below:

Do you feel rushed into being changed? What is the fruit of patience (see 2 Peter 3:9)?

How does delighting in the Lord and allowing Him to give you the desires of your heart give you peace just as you are right now (see Psalm 37:4)?

For the long jump exercise in the video, which option did you choose? To take a risk, or take it easy? How does this correlate to your exercise goal success in the way define it in the Lord?

What would your friends and family choose, and how does that impact the way they support you in your health journey for joy? How can you support them better as well?

4-Week Check-In

What have you learned about joyful movement so far?

How have you seen God working in you, and what are you working out (Phil 2:12)?

What in your life has changed, and how can you adapt your exercise plan or priorities for His Kingdom (Matthew 6:33)?

By Grace

Lord, thank you for teaching me...

WEEK OF: _____

Menu Sketch

Use the space below to brainstorm meal and snack ideas for the week and to create a grocery list. Don't worry about what day you will eat each item. Your appetite and schedule could change throughout the week. Taco Tuesday just might turn into Taco Monday, etc. If you need help, consult the other members of your household. Kids especially love to add their two cents.

Dinner Ideas   **GROCERY LIST**

1.

2.

3.

4.

5.

6.

Lunch Ideas

1.

2.

3.

Breakfast Ideas

1.

2.

3.

Snacks & Fun Foods

1.

2.

3.

WEEK OF: _____

Exercise Ideas

Use the space below to jot down ways you would like to exercise this week. If it helps you with logistics, fill in the week below with your plans. Make sure to schedule same muscle group strength sessions on non-consecutive days and include an active rest day. Use the FITT recommendations provided in the Introduction on page 6 to guide you, but feel free to change it up based on your body and day's needs.

What I already enjoy	**Cardio Ideas (3-5x/week)**
1.	1.
2.	2.
3.	3.
4.	4.
5.	5.

Strength Ideas (2-3x/week)	**Stretch/Mobility Ideas (2-7x/week)**
1.	1.
2.	2.
3.	3.

	Sun	Mon	Tues	Wed	Thurs	Fri	Sat
What I'm Already Doing							
How I can add strength							
How I can add cardio							
How I can add mobility							

DATE: _____

Proverbs 4:6-7 (NIV)

"Do not forsake wisdom and she will protect you; love her and she will watch over you. The beginning of wisdom is this: Get wisdom. Though it cost all you have, get understanding."

Today, I'm grateful for

Time	Hunger*	What I ate	Fullness*	Satisfaction*	Notes

Fitness Felt Need*	Time	Workout	Before	After	Notes

Rate hunger, fullness and satisfaction on scale of 1-10. Reference hunger/fullness scale and fitness felt needs on pages 5-6.

Other self-care I engaged in:

Prayer:

DATE: _____

Galatians 6:9

"And let us not grow weary of doing good, for in due season we will reap if we do not give up."

Today, I'm grateful for

Time	Hunger*	What I ate	Fullness*	Satisfaction*	Notes

Fitness Felt Need*	Time	Workout	Before	After	Notes

Rate hunger, fullness and satisfaction on scale of 1-10. Reference hunger/fullness scale and fitness felt needs on pages 5-6.

Other self-care I engaged in:

Prayer:

DATE: _____

2 Peter 3:9

"The Lord is not slow to fulfill his promise as some count slowness, but is patient toward you, not wishing that any should perish, but that all should reach repentance."

Today, I'm grateful for

Time	Hunger*	What I ate	Fullness*	Satisfaction*	Notes

Fitness Felt Need	Time	Workout	Before	After	Notes

Rate hunger, fullness and satisfaction on scale of 1-10. Reference hunger/fullness scale and fitness felt needs on pages 5-6.

Other self-care I engaged in:

Prayer:

Week Five

STRENGTH EXERCISE		Date	Date	Date	Date	Date	Notes
	Weight						
	Reps						
	Sets						
	RPE						
	Weight						
	Reps						
	Sets						
	RPE						
	Weight						
	Reps						
	Sets						
	RPE						
	Weight						
	Reps						
	Sets						
	RPE						
	Weight						
	Reps						
	Sets						
	RPE						
	Weight						
	Reps						
	Sets						
	RPE						
CARDIO EXERCISE		Date	Date	Date	Date	Date	Notes
	Time						
	Distance						
	Intensity*						
	Time						
	Distance						
	Intensity*						

RPE: 1-10 Rate of Perceived Exertion *Intensity: L/M/V Light/Moderate/Vigorous or HR

Week Six

Eat Well

▣ Enjoy God's Love Gift of Food

"Go, eat your bread with joy, and drink your wine with a merry heart, for God has already approved what you do." Ecclesiastes 9:7

After watching the video, "Enjoy God's Love Gift of Food," take time to answer the questions below:

What are your top ten favorite foods or meals to eat? If you're having a hard time with this, think back to childhood or a time before food rules took over your conscience.

Are there foods on that list that you loved as a child, but don't eat now? Why is that?

What positive memories do you have with food growing up? These might have to do with family traditions, friends, vacations, a specific relative, etc.

What are some ideas you have for adding more pleasure to your eating experiences? (Hint: this doesn't HAVE to be sweets/fun foods, it can be starting food traditions like Friday night family dinner, Saturday brunch, etc.; it could be about changing the aesthetics of the eating *environment* to add more enjoyment).

Move Free

📹 Modifying Movement for Your Mood

"Or do you presume on the riches of his kindness and forbearance and patience, not knowing that God's kindness is meant to lead you to repentance?" Romans 2:4

After watching the video, "Modifying Movement for Your Mood," take time to answer the questions below:

"Your word is a lamp to my feet and a light to my path." Psalm 119:105

Am I still on track with my Joy Goal, or has the Spirit led me in a new direction?

Do I need to change my motivator?

What changes do I notice in my body during my hormonal cycle?

Are there ways I am working against my body and feeling divided?

How does being kind to my body lead me to take care of myself as a reflection of loving God with a whole heart? How does this practice change my relationship with Him?

Do I need to do a body scan and take inventory of this temple of the Lord? Consider special places that need to be cared for, built up, rested, etc.

If so, here are my observations:

By Grace

Lord, thank you for teaching me...

WEEK OF: _____

Menu Sketch

Use the space below to brainstorm meal and snack ideas for the week and to create a grocery list. Don't worry about what day you will eat each item. Your appetite and schedule could change throughout the week. Taco Tuesday just might turn into Taco Monday, etc. If you need help, consult the other members of your household. Kids especially love to add their two cents.

Dinner Ideas   **GROCERY LIST**

1.

2.

3.

4.

5.

6.

Lunch Ideas

1.

2.

3.

Breakfast Ideas

1.

2.

3.

Snacks & Fun Foods

1.

2.

3.

WEEK OF:_____

Exercise Ideas

Use the space below to jot down ways you would like to exercise this week. If it helps you with logistics, fill in the week below with your plans. Make sure to schedule same muscle group strength sessions on non-consecutive days and include an active rest day. Use the FITT recommendations provided in the Introduction on page 6 to guide you, but feel free to change it up based on your body and day's needs.

What I already enjoy
1.
2.
3.
4.
5.

Cardio Ideas (3-5x/week)
1.
2.
3.
4.
5.

Strength Ideas (2-3x/week)
1.
2.
3.

Stretch/Mobility Ideas (2-7x/week)
1.
2.
3.

	Sun	Mon	Tues	Wed	Thurs	Fri	Sat
What I'm Already Doing							
How I can add strength							
How I can add cardio							
How I can add mobility							

DATE: ───────────────────

Ecclesiastes 9:7

"Go, eat your bread with joy, and drink your wine with a merry heart, for God has already approved what you do."

Today, I'm grateful for

Time	Hunger*	What I ate	Fullness*	Satisfaction*	Notes

Fitness Felt Need*	Time	Workout	Before	After	Notes

Rate hunger, fullness and satisfaction on scale of 1-10. Reference hunger/fullness scale and fitness felt needs on pages 5-6.

Other self-care I engaged in:

Prayer:

DATE: _____

Romans 2:4

"Or do you presume on the riches of his kindness and forbearance and patience, not knowing that God's kindness is meant to lead you to repentance?"

Today, I'm grateful for

Time	Hunger*	What I ate	Fullness*	Satisfaction*	Notes

Fitness Felt Need*	Time	Workout	Before	After	Notes

Rate hunger, fullness and satisfaction on scale of 1-10. Reference hunger/fullness scale and fitness felt needs on pages 5-6.

Other self-care I engaged in:

Prayer:

DATE: _____

Psalm 119:105
"Your Word is a lamp to my feet and a light to my path."

Today, I'm grateful for

Time	Hunger*	What I ate	Fullness*	Satisfaction*	Notes

Fitness Felt Need	Time	Workout	Before	After	Notes

Rate hunger, fullness and satisfaction on scale of 1-10. Reference hunger/fullness scale and fitness felt needs on pages 5-6.

Other self-care I engaged in:

Prayer:

STRENGTH EXERCISE		Date	Date	Date	Date	Date	Notes
	Weight						
	Reps						
	Sets						
	RPE						
	Weight						
	Reps						
	Sets						
	RPE						
	Weight						
	Reps						
	Sets						
	RPE						
	Weight						
	Reps						
	Sets						
	RPE						
	Weight						
	Reps						
	Sets						
	RPE						
	Weight						
	Reps						
	Sets						
	RPE						
CARDIO EXERCISE		Date	Date	Date	Date	Date	Notes
	Time						
	Distance						
	Intensity*						
	Time						
	Distance						
	Intensity*						

RPE: 1-10 Rate of Perceived Exertion*Intensity: L/M/V Light/Moderate/Vigorous or HR

Week Seven

Eat Well

📽 Practicing Thanksgiving vs. Judgement with Food

"Do not be anxious about anything, but in everything by prayer and supplication with thanksgiving let your requests be made known to God. And the peace of God, which surpasses all understanding, will guard your hearts and your minds in Christ Jesus." Philippians 4:6-7

After watching the video, "Practicing Thanksgiving vs. Judgement with Food," take time to answer the questions below:

Choose one meal or snack time each day for the next week to practice mindful gratitude. Aim for a meal or snack where you will have the time and space to sit down and shut out distractions. You don't need an hour. Fifteen minutes should be plenty. Which meal did you choose?

Go through the following steps/questions during your mindful meal.

A MINDFUL MEAL WITH CHRIST

a) Sit down with your food and shut off your phone. Take 3 deep belly breaths to activate the parasympathetic nervous system. Inhale God's grace and love, exhale all the shame and fears from the day.

b) Take a moment to notice the appearance of your food, the colors, textures, maybe even anything pleasant about the environment around you. Notice the smell of the food.

c) Give thanks to God for the good things you see, the blessings of this day and the food in front of you. Thank him for the freedom in Christ to enjoy all foods and to partake in His health, purchased for you on the cross.

d) Eat your food and enjoy it (YAY!). If you start to notice judgement rising up about a certain food, stop and remember: All food is made clean by the word of Christ and thanksgiving. Redirect judgement to curiosity. How does it taste? What on my plate am I most craving? Am I enjoying this food or not? How is it providing positive nourishment for me?

e) About midway through eating your food, stop and ask the questions above. Assess how full you are feeling. This does not mean you have to stop eating. It's simply to bring awareness to your fullness/satisfaction level. Keep eating until you are confident you will be full and satisfied until the next meal. Get more food if you aren't full at the end!

f) After completing the mindful meal for a few days to a week, write about your experience. Did you notice increased satisfaction/fullness? Did you learn something else about yourself and your eating? Describe below.

Move Free

🎥 Exposing the Enemies of Distraction and Shame

"...[W]ho for the joy that was set before him endured the cross, despising the shame, and is seated at the right hand of the throne of God." Hebrews 12:2

After watching the video, "Exposing the Enemies of Distraction and Shame," take time to answer the questions below:

What are you ashamed of in your fitness journey? Example: Not knowing how to use equipment leads to fear of the gym and internally blaming yourself for ignorance, or others for not teaching you. Maybe it's something deeper. Name it here:

Adam and Eve were afraid of being seen naked, so they covered themselves up with fig leaves (Genesis 3:10). What are you afraid of that shame exposing, and how do you cover up?

How does this fear cause you to shrink back, and what kind of freedom could you be missing out on?

"There is no fear in love, but perfect love casts out fear. For fear has to do with punishment, and whoever fears has not been perfected in love." 1 John 4:18

Psalm 34:5 says, "Those who look to him are radiant, and their faces shall never be ashamed." How can you look to Jesus instead? How does the shift from yourself to a focus on Him draw you out in joy, the way your arms extend out from your body in movement?

What in your fitness journey are you blaming yourself for, and how are you trying to fix it yourself? Would you like to give it to Jesus in prayer instead?

"as far as the east is from the west,
so far does he remove our transgressions from us.
As a father shows compassion to his children,
so the Lord shows compassion to those who fear him." Psalm 103:12-13

Write down one clear goal for exercise this week.

Are you receiving feedback if the workout is too hard or too easy? How can you adjust to find your flow?

How can you progress your goal in a way that feels exciting for you?

How is your Joy Goal compelling you, and how is exercising supporting your identity formation in this season?

By Grace

Lord, thank you for teaching me...

WEEK OF: _____

Menu Sketch

Use the space below to brainstorm meal and snack ideas for the week and to create a grocery list. Don't worry about what day you will eat each item. Your appetite and schedule could change throughout the week. Taco Tuesday just might turn into Taco Monday, etc. If you need help, consult the other members of your household. Kids especially love to add their two cents.

Dinner Ideas

1.

2.

3.

4.

5.

6.

Lunch Ideas

1.

2.

3.

Breakfast Ideas

1.

2.

3.

Snacks & Fun Foods

1.

2.

3.

GROCERY LIST

WEEK OF:_____

Exercise Ideas

Use the space below to jot down ways you would like to exercise this week. If it helps you with logistics, fill in the week below with your plans. Make sure to schedule same muscle group strength sessions on non-consecutive days and include an active rest day. Use the FITT recommendations provided in the Introduction on page 6 to guide you, but feel free to change it up based on your body and day's needs.

What I already enjoy
1.
2.
3.
4.
5.

Cardio Ideas (3-5x/week)
1.
2.
3.
4.
5.

Strength Ideas (2-3x/week)
1.
2.
3.

Stretch/Mobility Ideas (2-7x/week)
1.
2.
3.

	Sun	Mon	Tues	Wed	Thurs	Fri	Sat
What I'm Already Doing							
How I can add strength							
How I can add cardio							
How I can add mobility							

DATE: _____

Philippians 4:6

"Do not be anxious about anything, but in everything by prayer and supplication with thanksgiving, let your requests be made known to God."

Today, I'm grateful for

Time	Hunger*	What I ate	Fullness*	Satisfaction*	Notes

Fitness Felt Need*	Time	Workout	Before	After	Notes

Rate hunger, fullness and satisfaction on scale of 1-10. Reference hunger/fullness scale and fitness felt needs on pages 5-6.

Other self-care I engaged in:

Prayer:

DATE: _____

Hebrews 12:2

"…[W]ho for the joy that was set before him, endured the cross, despising the shame, and is seated at the right hand of the throne of God."

Today, I'm grateful for

Time	Hunger*	What I ate	Fullness*	Satisfaction*	Notes

Fitness Felt Need*	Time	Workout	Before	After	Notes

Rate hunger, fullness and satisfaction on scale of 1-10. Reference hunger/fullness scale and fitness felt needs on pages 5-6.

Other self-care I engaged in:

Prayer:

DATE: _____

Psalm 34:5
"Those who look to him are radiant, and their faces shall never be ashamed."

Today, I'm grateful for

Time	Hunger*	What I ate	Fullness*	Satisfaction*	Notes

Fitness Felt Need	Time	Workout	Before	After	Notes

Rate hunger, fullness and satisfaction on scale of 1-10. Reference hunger/fullness scale and fitness felt needs on pages 5-6.

Other self-care I engaged in:

Prayer:

STRENGTH EXERCISE		Date	Date	Date	Date	Date	Date
	Weight						
	Reps						
	Sets						
	RPE						
	Weight						
	Reps						
	Sets						
	RPE						
	Weight						
	Reps						
	Sets						
	RPE						
	Weight						
	Reps						
	Sets						
	RPE						
	Weight						
	Reps						
	Sets						
	RPE						
	Weight						
	Reps						
	Sets						
	RPE						
CARDIO EXERCISE		Date	Date	Date	Date	Date	Date
	Time						
	Distance						
	Intensity*						
	Time						
	Distance						
	Intensity*						

RPE: 1-10 Rate of Perceived Exertion*Intensity: L/M/V Light/Moderate/Vigorous or HR

Week Eight

Eat Well

📹 Discerning Spirit-Led Health Changes

"We destroy arguments and every lofty opinion raised against the knowledge of God, and take every thought captive to obey Christ…" 2 Corinthians 10:5

After watching the video, "Discerning Spirit-Led Health Changes," take time to answer the questions below:

Have you ever made a health change motivated by fear, shame or comparison? Describe that change, and the results:

God knows we are only human, so He often works by transforming one small area of your life at a time, one habit. He doesn't often ask you to completely revamp everything you're doing, but rather begins to change your heart and prepare you for action in one area. With this in mind, can you think of any health changes you've felt gentle nudges about making?

Why do you feel making this health change would be helpful?

Do you have any beginning ideas for how you can make this change?

📹 Forming Habits and Rhythms with the Spirit

"For it is God who works in you, both to will and to work for his good pleasure."
Philippians 2:13

"No discipline seems pleasant at the time, but painful. Later on, however, it produces a harvest of righteousness and peace for those who have been trained by it." Hebrews 12:11

After watching the video, "Forming Habits and Rhythms with The Spirit," take time to answer the questions below:

Describe goals you have set in the past. Which goals have provided long term change and which ones have left no impact? Why do you think that is?

After going through the last section on discerning Spirit-led health changes, what habit/rhythm is God calling you to focus on (please pick only one or two)? Note this does not have to be food or exercise related.

How regularly will you perform this habit? Daily? Weekly? Monthly? And when will you perform it?

Is there anything you need to learn, lookup, purchase, or do before you are able to start practicing this habit/rhythm?

Is this habit/rhythm something that will be healthy and doable for a lifetime or this season of your life? Or is it something you don't want to be doing 3 months from now?

Look ahead to the future, 3 months, 1 year, 5 years from now, ask God to show you how forming this habit or rhythm will complete your joy. Describe what you envision below.

Move Free

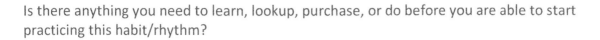 Training Persistence and Patience

"Consider him who endured from sinners such hostility against himself, so that you may not grow weary or fainthearted." Hebrews 12:3

After watching the video, "Training Persistence and Patience," take time to answer the questions below:

What was your original motivation to start this course?

"Motivation" is temporary, but hope lasts because hope is dependent on the Spirit and rooted in memory. What has God already done in you? Record your testimony:

How is God growing your hope through this journey by stepping back from old habits to make room for the Spirit to lead?

Where in your life is willpower not enough?

Do you need to reach the point of your own failure before you can rest your heart in God's power? If so, how can God become your strength in weakness?

"My flesh and my heart may fail, but God is the strength of my heart and my portion forever." Psalm 73:26

What movements and habits are becoming more like an extension of your own body?

Write a prayer of thanksgiving to Jesus, that He prepared the way, is with you now, and always will be:

By Grace

Lord, thank you for teaching me...

WEEK OF: _____

Menu Sketch

Use the space below to brainstorm meal and snack ideas for the week and to create a grocery list. Don't worry about what day you will eat each item. Your appetite and schedule could change throughout the week. Taco Tuesday just might turn into Taco Monday, etc. If you need help, consult the other members of your household. Kids especially love to add their two cents.

Dinner Ideas   **GROCERY LIST**

1.

2.

3.

4.

5.

6.

Lunch Ideas

1.

2.

3.

Breakfast Ideas

1.

2.

3.

Snacks & Fun Foods

1.

2.

3.

WEEK OF: _____

Exercise Ideas

Use the space below to jot down ways you would like to exercise this week. If it helps you with logistics, fill in the week below with your plans. Make sure to schedule same muscle group strength sessions on non-consecutive days and include an active rest day. Use the FITT recommendations provided in the Introduction on page 6 to guide you, but feel free to change it up based on your body and day's needs.

What I already enjoy
1.
2.
3.
4.
5.

Cardio Ideas (3-5x/week)
1.
2.
3.
4.
5.

Strength Ideas (2-3x/week)
1.
2.
3.

Stretch/Mobility Ideas (2-7x/week)
1.
2.
3.

	Sun	Mon	Tues	Wed	Thurs	Fri	Sat
What I'm Already Doing							
How I can add strength							
How I can add cardio							
How I can add mobility							

DATE: _____

2 Corinthians 10:5

"We destroy arguments and every lofty opinion raised against the knowledge of God, and take every thought captive to obey Christ…"

Today, I'm grateful for

Time	Hunger*	What I ate	Fullness*	Satisfaction*	Notes

Fitness Felt Need*	Time	Workout	Before	After	Notes

Rate hunger, fullness and satisfaction on scale of 1-10. Reference hunger/fullness scale and fitness felt needs on pages 5-6.

Other self-care I engaged in:

Prayer:

DATE: _____

Philippians 2:13

"For it is God who works in you, both to will and to work for his good pleasure."

Today, I'm grateful for

Time	Hunger*	What I ate	Fullness*	Satisfaction*	Notes

Fitness Felt Need*	Time	Workout	Before	After	Notes

Rate hunger, fullness and satisfaction on scale of 1-10. Reference hunger/fullness scale and fitness felt needs on pages 5-6.

Other self-care I engaged in:

Prayer:

DATE: _____

Hebrews 12:13

"Consider him who endured from sinners such hostility against himself, so that you may not grow weary or fainthearted."

Today, I'm grateful for

Time	Hunger*	What I ate	Fullness*	Satisfaction*	Notes

Fitness Felt Need	Time	Workout	Before	After	Notes

Rate hunger, fullness and satisfaction on scale of 1-10. Reference hunger/fullness scale and fitness felt needs on pages 5-6.

Other self-care I engaged in:

Prayer:

STRENGTH EXERCISE		Date	Date	Date	Date	Date	Date
	Weight						
	Reps						
	Sets						
	RPE						
	Weight						
	Reps						
	Sets						
	RPE						
	Weight						
	Reps						
	Sets						
	RPE						
	Weight						
	Reps						
	Sets						
	RPE						
	Weight						
	Reps						
	Sets						
	RPE						
	Weight						
	Reps						
	Sets						
	RPE						
CARDIO EXERCISE		Date	Date	Date	Date	Date	Date
	Time						
	Distance						
	Intensity*						
	Time						
	Distance						
	Intensity*						

RPE: 1-10 Rate of Perceived Exertion*Intensity: L/M/V Light/Moderate/Vigorous or HR

MONTH OF:_____

Joyful Health at a Glance

SUN	MON	TUES	WED	THURS	FRI	SAT

Week Nine

Eat Well

🎥 The Truth Behind Emotional Eating and Food Addiction

"For God gave us a spirit not of fear but of power and love and self-control." 2 Timothy 1:7

After watching the video, "The Truth Behind Emotional Eating and Food Addiction," take time to answer the questions below:

Have you ever thought of yourself as an emotional eater? What does that term mean to you?

Think of some instances where emotional eating could be a positive experience:

If you feel that you eat emotionally in excess...
When does it most often happen?

How can you ensure you are properly fueled leading up to the triggering event?

Are there any specific foods you eat during this time? Have you worked through this food as a "fear food" yet? What are some positive nutritional qualities of this food?

What do you feel you truly need in this situation? (Maybe it's to talk to a friend, journal with the Lord, go on a walk, get some sleep, etc.)

Are there any foods that you have thought of as addicting in the past? How does the information in this video affect how you view that food addiction now?

What might be some reasons you found that food addicting?

Spend some time asking God to show you how you can care for physical and emotional health in a way that gets to the root of your hurt and improves your relationship with food & body.

Move Free

📷 Self-Discipline is Self-Care

"For the moment all discipline seems painful rather than pleasant, but later it yields the peaceful fruit of righteousness to those who have been trained by it."
Hebrews 12:11

After watching the video, "Self-Discipline is Self-Care," take time to answer the questions below:

What is your idea of spiritual discipline?

What is your idea of physical self-care?

How can moving for joy in the Lord reconcile the two?

Reevaluation: What has been successful thus far? How have things changed? What do you need to change? Consider writing down how the Lord has helped you as a reminder for how He will (see 1 Samuel 7:12):

Identity & Body Image

📽 Seeing Who God Sees in the Mirror

"For the Lord sees not as man sees: man looks on the outward appearance, but the Lord looks on the heart." 1 Samuel 16:7

After watching the video, "Seeing Who God Sees in the Mirror," take time to answer the questions below:

What do you typically see when you look in the mirror?
   a) Parts of your body you'd like to fix
   b) Yourself, smiling back
   c) An outside shell that doesn't reflect the real you
   d) Someone you can't stand looking at
   e) Other:

What does good body image mean to you? Is there a certain type of body you have felt you needed in order to have good body image? Describe in detail:

Where did you get that picture from? How has each of the following contributed to this picture?

Family:

Friends:

Facebook (social media):

When did you feel unloved that made you self-aware and fixated on improving a part of your body, or like you didn't belong?

When you're having a "bad body image day" what often triggers it? Think beyond looking a certain way or weighing a certain number (although the scale can be a trigger). Are you nervous about meeting new people? Afraid for a job interview, etc.?

Has exercise played a role in achieving that ideal body image? If so, how?

What ways have you tried to cope with body image in the past? How can you use connection to cope in a healthier way in the future?

Consider these verses:

"Therefore, if anyone is in Christ, he is a new creation. The old has passed away; behold, the new has come." 2 Corinthians 5:17

"And we, who with unveiled faces all reflect the glory of the Lord, are being transformed into His image with intensifying glory, which comes from the Lord, who is the Spirit." 2 Corinthians 3:18

"You are altogether beautiful, my love; there is no flaw in you." Song of Solomon 4:7

Ask God how He sees you, and write down anything more He might reveal here:

How can God's truth open your eyes to the reality of what He sees? Consider the verses:

Live by faith: "I have been crucified with Christ. It is no longer I who live, but Christ who lives in me. And the life I now live in the flesh I live by faith in the Son of God, who loved me and gave himself for me." Galatians 2:20

Look to God: "As for me, I shall behold your face in righteousness; when I awake, I shall be satisfied with your likeness." Psalm 17:15

Speak truth: "Instead, speaking the truth in love, we will grow to become in every respect the mature body of him who is the head, that is, Christ." Ephesians 4:15

Write down a prayer in response:

By Grace

Lord, thank you for teaching me...

WEEK OF: _____

Menu Sketch

Use the space below to brainstorm meal and snack ideas for the week and to create a grocery list. Don't worry about what day you will eat each item. Your appetite and schedule could change throughout the week. Taco Tuesday just might turn into Taco Monday, etc. If you need help, consult the other members of your household. Kids especially love to add their two cents.

Dinner Ideas

1.
2.
3.
4.
5.
6.

Lunch Ideas

1.
2.
3.

Breakfast Ideas

1.
2.
3.

Snacks & Fun Foods

1.
2.
3.

GROCERY LIST

WEEK OF: _____

Exercise Ideas

Use the space below to jot down ways you would like to exercise this week. If it helps you with logistics, fill in the week below with your plans. Make sure to schedule same muscle group strength sessions on non-consecutive days and include an active rest day. Use the FITT recommendations provided in the Introduction on page 6 to guide you, but feel free to change it up based on your body and day's needs.

What I already enjoy
1.
2.
3.
4.
5.

Cardio Ideas (3-5x/week)
1.
2.
3.
4.
5.

Strength Ideas (2-3x/week)
1.
2.
3.

Stretch/Mobility Ideas (2-7x/week)
1.
2.
3.

	Sun	Mon	Tues	Wed	Thurs	Fri	Sat
What I'm Already Doing							
How I can add strength							
How I can add cardio							
How I can add mobility							

DATE: _____

2 Timothy 1:7

"For God gave us a Spirit not of fear but of power and love and self-control."

Today, I'm grateful for

Time	Hunger*	What I ate	Fullness*	Satisfaction*	Notes

Fitness Felt Need*	Time	Workout	Before	After	Notes

Rate hunger, fullness and satisfaction on scale of 1-10. Reference hunger/fullness scale and fitness felt needs on pages 5-6.

Other self-care I engaged in:

Prayer:

DATE: _____

Hebrews 12:11

"For the moment all discipline seems painful rather than pleasant, but later it yields the peaceful fruit of righteousness to those who have been trained by it."

Today, I'm grateful for

Time	Hunger*	What I ate	Fullness*	Satisfaction*	Notes

Fitness Felt Need*	Time	Workout	Before	After	Notes

*Rate hunger, fullness and satisfaction on scale of 1-10. Reference hunger/fullness scale and fitness felt needs on pages 5-6.

Other self-care I engaged in:

Prayer:

DATE: _____

1 Samuel 16:7

"For the Lord sees not as man sees: man looks on the outward appearance, but the Lord looks on the heart."

Today, I'm grateful for

Time	Hunger*	What I ate	Fullness*	Satisfaction*	Notes

Fitness Felt Need	Time	Workout	Before	After	Notes

Rate hunger, fullness and satisfaction on scale of 1-10. Reference hunger/fullness scale and fitness felt needs on pages 5-6.

Other self-care I engaged in:

Prayer:

STRENGTH EXERCISE		Date	Date	Date	Date	Date	Date
	Weight						
	Reps						
	Sets						
	RPE						
	Weight						
	Reps						
	Sets						
	RPE						
	Weight						
	Reps						
	Sets						
	RPE						
	Weight						
	Reps						
	Sets						
	RPE						
	Weight						
	Reps						
	Sets						
	RPE						
	Weight						
	Reps						
	Sets						
	RPE						
CARDIO EXERCISE		Date	Date	Date	Date	Date	Date
	Time						
	Distance						
	Intensity*						
	Time						
	Distance						
	Intensity*						

RPE: 1-10 Rate of Perceived Exertion*Intensity: L/M/V Light/Moderate/Vigorous or HR

Week Ten

Eat Well

📽 Meal Planning Without Rigidity

"The heart of man plans his way, but the Lord establishes his steps." Proverbs 16:9

After watching the video, "Meal Planning Without Rigidity," take time to answer the questions below:

When you think of meal/menu planning, what comes to mind?

Are you someone who has enjoyed meal/menu planning in the past? What's worked for you, what hasn't?

What mindset shift/strategy from the video can you employ to help meal planning become more helpful and less stressful?

Use the questions below to help to brainstorm meal and snack ideas for the week. Then move your ideas to the weekly meal planning template provided at the end of each week's content.

Starting with dinners, how many will you likely eat at home this week? Pick mainly meals that you can make quickly from memory, include a maximum of 1-2 meals that take more effort or thought.

Move on to lunch. If you can, try to utilize dinner leftovers, and then brainstorm 2-3 quick fix lunch ideas outside of leftovers.

Next, brainstorm 2-3 breakfast ideas.

Finally, list out snack ideas and fun foods you want to include this week.

If applicable, how can you get your family involved in the planning? How can you add more pleasure and fun to your meal plan?

Remember this is simply a brain dump of ideas to help you plan and grocery shop. You do not have to have Tuesday's meal on Tuesday, if you decide you actually want Wednesday's meal that day, etc. The key is to plan meals that are pleasurable and doable instead of shooting for "food perfection." If you are having a hard time thinking of ideas, make sure to consult other members of your household first, then think of easy staple meals you can make from memory, and lastly, go to the internet or recipe books for inspiration.

Move Free

📽 When You Don't Feel Like Moving

"Lift up your hands to the holy place and bless the LORD!" Psalm 134:2

After watching the video, "When You Don't Feel Like Moving," take time to answer the questions below:

Identify the times when you really don't feel like exercising:

a.

b.

c.

d.

What is your heart saying in those moments? Do you feel driven to exercise by fear? Consider resting. Do you feel led by love? Follow His lead! In the answers above, write down if you feel the voice of fear or love speaking, and the appropriate response. Write down any other thoughts below:

When have you moved even when you didn't want to, and still experienced the benefits? How can lifting your hands in worship help elevate your spiritual heart as well?

What is a go-to movement that is always helpful for you?

How can you put exercise in the way of your life, or make exercise a natural part of your day?

By Grace

Lord, thank you for teaching me...

WEEK OF: _____

Menu Sketch

Use the space below to brainstorm meal and snack ideas for the week and to create a grocery list. Don't worry about what day you will eat each item. Your appetite and schedule could change throughout the week. Taco Tuesday just might turn into Taco Monday, etc. If you need help, consult the other members of your household. Kids especially love to add their two cents.

Dinner Ideas

1.
2.
3.
4.
5.
6.

Lunch Ideas

1.
2.
3.

Breakfast Ideas

1.
2.
3.

Snacks & Fun Foods

1.
2.
3.

GROCERY LIST

WEEK OF: _____

Exercise Ideas

Use the space below to jot down ways you would like to exercise this week. If it helps you with logistics, fill in the week below with your plans. Make sure to schedule same muscle group strength sessions on non-consecutive days and include an active rest day. Use the FITT recommendations provided in the Introduction on page 6 to guide you, but feel free to change it up based on your body and day's needs.

What I already enjoy
1.
2.
3.
4.
5.

Cardio Ideas (3-5x/week)
1.
2.
3.
4.
5.

Strength Ideas (2-3x/week)
1.
2.
3.

Stretch/Mobility Ideas (2-7x/week)
1.
2.
3.

	Sun	Mon	Tues	Wed	Thurs	Fri	Sat
What I'm Already Doing							
How I can add strength							
How I can add cardio							
How I can add mobility							

DATE: _____

Proverbs 16:9

"The heart of man plans his way, but the Lord establishes his steps."

Today, I'm grateful for

Time	Hunger*	What I ate	Fullness*	Satisfaction*	Notes

Fitness Felt Need*	Time	Workout	Before	After	Notes

Rate hunger, fullness and satisfaction on scale of 1-10. Reference hunger/fullness scale and fitness felt needs on pages 5-6.

Other self-care I engaged in:

Prayer:

DATE: _____

Psalm 134:2

"Lift up your hands to the holy place and bless the LORD!"

Today, I'm grateful for

Time	Hunger*	What I ate	Fullness*	Satisfaction*	Notes

Fitness Felt Need*	Time	Workout	Before	After	Notes

Rate hunger, fullness and satisfaction on scale of 1-10. Reference hunger/fullness scale and fitness felt needs on pages 5-6.

Other self-care I engaged in:

Prayer:

DATE: _____

2 Corinthians 5:17

"Therefore, if anyone is in Christ, he is a new creation. The old has passed away; behold, the new has come."

Today, I'm grateful for

Time	Hunger*	What I ate	Fullness*	Satisfaction*	Notes

Fitness Felt Need	Time	Workout	Before	After	Notes

Rate hunger, fullness and satisfaction on scale of 1-10. Reference hunger/fullness scale and fitness felt needs on pages 5-6.

Other self-care I engaged in:

Prayer:

STRENGTH EXERCISE		Date	Date	Date	Date	Date	Date
	Weight						
	Reps						
	Sets						
	RPE						
	Weight						
	Reps						
	Sets						
	RPE						
	Weight						
	Reps						
	Sets						
	RPE						
	Weight						
	Reps						
	Sets						
	RPE						
	Weight						
	Reps						
	Sets						
	RPE						
	Weight						
	Reps						
	Sets						
	RPE						
CARDIO EXERCISE		Date	Date	Date	Date	Date	Date
	Time						
	Distance						
	Intensity*						
	Time						
	Distance						
	Intensity*						

RPE: 1-10 Rate of Perceived Exertion*Intensity: L/M/V Light/Moderate/Vigorous

Week Eleven

Eat Well

🎥 Creating a Grace Fueled Food Culture at Home

"On this mountain the Lord Almighty will prepare a feast of rich food for all peoples, a banquet of aged wine—the best of meats and the finest of wines." Isaiah 25: 6

"For I was hungry and you gave me something to eat, I was thirsty and you gave me something to drink, I was a stranger and you invited me in," Matthew 25:35

After watching the video, "Creating a Grace Fueled Food Culture at Home," take time to answer the questions below:

Envision your family or household 5 to 10 years from now. How do you want to relate to food with your loved ones? What memories do you want to make? What do you hope your kids remember about food and their childhood?

What traditions do you have around food currently? Do you and/or your family enjoy these traditions and look forward to them?

What traditions do you want to start surrounding food (Friday night family dinners, Saturday morning donuts, Sunday brunch, etc)?

How can you involve your family/friends in food preparation and planning?

In what ways can you practice hospitality/caring for others with food regularly?

If you have children, or want to in the future, what concerns do you have about feeding them?

After watching the video and/or reviewing Ellyn Satter's Division of responsibility* with food, is there anything you want to implement in how you feed your children?
*Parents are in charge of what is offered, when, and where kids eat, Children are in charge of what they eat and whether they eat

Finally, how can you change the food/body talk in your household? Are there any conversations you need to have with loved ones? Ask the Lord for guidance and remembrance in this area.

Move Free

🎥 Exercising With Your People

"And after [Lydia] was baptized, and her household as well, she urged us, saying, 'If you have judged me to be faithful to the Lord, come to my house and stay.' And she prevailed upon us." Acts 16:15

After watching the video, "Exercising With Your People," take time to answer the questions below:

What exercise is fun for you, and how can you invite your people to join you?

Think about those who live with or around you. How can you discover what they like to do for exercise? Consider how you can experience this with them. How would this bring you closer?

Ask your family and/or friends how they would like to be active together this week. You could give them options and let them choose if they are a blank slate. Walking is always a great go-to, as is bike riding, taking a fitness class together, or video game fitness. If you have kids, they always have good ideas. No matter how goofy they might be, go with it! List them here, and circle one you'll do this week:

a.

b.

c.

d.

e.

f.

Are there any ways you can serve together with movement? Think Habitat for Humanity, walking to a store and buying someone's groceries, doing yardwork for an elderly neighbor, or taking kids for a bike ride to give mom a break. List one thing you will do together this month:

Now, dream big! What are some things you could do together that would be more adventurous, more of a weekend outing or vacation activity? Think hiking a new location, bike riding at the beach, or signing up for a destination race. List one thing you would like to do this year:

By Grace

Lord, thank you for teaching me...

WEEK OF: _____

Menu Sketch

Use the space below to brainstorm meal and snack ideas for the week and to create a grocery list. Don't worry about what day you will eat each item. Your appetite and schedule could change throughout the week. Taco Tuesday just might turn into Taco Monday, etc. If you need help, consult the other members of your household. Kids especially love to add their two cents.

Dinner Ideas

1.

2.

3.

4.

5.

6.

Lunch Ideas

1.

2.

3.

Breakfast Ideas

1.

2.

3.

Snacks & Fun Foods

1.

2.

3.

GROCERY LIST

WEEK OF: _____

Exercise Ideas

Use the space below to jot down ways you would like to exercise this week. If it helps you with logistics, fill in the week below with your plans. Make sure to schedule same muscle group strength sessions on non-consecutive days and include an active rest day. Use the FITT recommendations provided in the Introduction on page 6 to guide you, but feel free to change it up based on your body and day's needs.

What I already enjoy

1.
2.
3.
4.
5.

Cardio Ideas (3-5x/week)

1.
2.
3.
4.
5.

Strength Ideas (2-3x/week)

1.
2.
3.

Stretch/Mobility Ideas (2-7x/week)

1.
2.
3.

	Sun	Mon	Tues	Wed	Thurs	Fri	Sat
What I'm Already Doing							
How I can add strength							
How I can add cardio							
How I can add mobility							

DATE: _____

Isaiah 25:6

"On this mountain the Lord of hosts will make for all peoples a feast of rich food, a feast of well-aged wine, of rich food full of marrow, of aged wine well refined."

Today, I'm grateful for

Time	Hunger*	What I ate	Fullness*	Satisfaction*	Notes

Fitness Felt Need*	Time	Workout	Before	After	Notes

Rate hunger, fullness and satisfaction on scale of 1-10. Reference hunger/fullness scale and fitness felt needs on pages 5-6.

Other self-care I engaged in:

Prayer:

DATE: _____

Matthew 25:35

"For I was hungry and you gave me food, I was thirsty and you gave me drink, I was a stranger and you welcomed me,"

Today, I'm grateful for

Time	Hunger*	What I ate	Fullness*	Satisfaction*	Notes

Fitness Felt Need*	Time	Workout	Before	After	Notes

*Rate hunger, fullness and satisfaction on scale of 1-10. Reference hunger/fullness scale and fitness felt needs on pages 5-6.

Other self-care I engaged in:

Prayer:

DATE: _____

Acts 16:15

"And after she was baptized, and her household as well, she urged us, saying, 'If you have judged me to be faithful to the Lord, come to my house and stay.' And she prevailed upon us."

Today, I'm grateful for

Time	Hunger*	What I ate	Fullness*	Satisfaction*	Notes

Fitness Felt Need	Time	Workout	Before	After	Notes

Rate hunger, fullness and satisfaction on scale of 1-10. Reference hunger/fullness scale and fitness felt needs on pages 5-6.

Other self-care I engaged in:

Prayer:

STRENGTH EXERCISE	Date	Date	Date	Date	Date	Date

	Weight						
	Reps						
	Sets						
	RPE						
	Weight						
	Reps						
	Sets						
	RPE						
	Weight						
	Reps						
	Sets						
	RPE						
	Weight						
	Reps						
	Sets						
	RPE						
	Weight						
	Reps						
	Sets						
	RPE						
	Weight						
	Reps						
	Sets						
	RPE						
CARDIO EXERCISE		Date	Date	Date	Date	Date	Date
	Time						
	Distance						
	Intensity*						
	Time						
	Distance						
	Intensity*						

RPE: 1-10 Rate of Perceived Exertion*Intensity: L/M/V Light/Moderate/Vigorous or HR

Week Twelve

Eat Well

📹 Remaining Grace Fueled in Diet Culture

"So faith comes from hearing, and hearing through the word of Christ." Romans 10:17

"Finally, brothers and sisters, whatever is true, whatever is noble, whatever is right, whatever is pure, whatever is lovely, whatever is admirable—if anything is excellent or praiseworthy—think about such things." Philippians 4:8 (NIV)

After watching the video, "Remaining Grace Fueled in Diet Culture," take time to answer the questions below:

How has God changed the way you view and interact with food through this course?

What positive changes are you most confident about?

In what areas do you need to continue to remember God's grace? How will you fill your mind with what is lovely and true?

What boundaries are you setting for yourself and your family to help keep you grace fueled in diet-culture?

Look back at the Introduction questions and compare your answers. What was your hope for this course, and has the Lord transformed you throughout these twelve weeks?

Move Free

📽 Next Steps with the Lord

"For while bodily training is of some value, godliness is of value in every way, as it holds promise for the present life and also for the life to come." 1 Timothy 4:8

After watching the video, "Next Steps with The Lord," take time to answer the questions below:

Where in your fitness life does freedom, responsibility, and love feel out of balance with each other?

Is there anything you need to repent of fitness-wise, any fear you need to turn your back on, and be free to move in love?

Reviewing your motivator's transformation path (refer to Appendix A), what has maturity in godly training looked like for you?

How does "getting back on track" vs "staying in step with the Spirit" change your exercise journey going forward?

How are you going to check in with the Lord on your fitness journey? At the end of each month, or each season of your life?

List local resources you can turn to if you need extra help (pastors, personal trainers, physical therapists):

You're never alone in this journey. You're part of the body of Christ! Continue connecting with God in your heart and consider those He has put in your life to share exercise with. If you can't think of anyone, write down a prayer asking the Lord of the harvest to raise up others to walk with you, and write down any names that come up.

By Grace

Lord, thank you for teaching me...

WEEK OF: _____

Menu Sketch

Use the space below to brainstorm meal and snack ideas for the week and to create a grocery list. Don't worry about what day you will eat each item. Your appetite and schedule could change throughout the week. Taco Tuesday just might turn into Taco Monday, etc. If you need help, consult the other members of your household. Kids especially love to add their two cents.

Dinner Ideas

1.

2.

3.

4.

5.

6.

Lunch Ideas

1.

2.

3.

Breakfast Ideas

1.

2.

3.

Snacks & Fun Foods

1.

2.

3.

GROCERY LIST

WEEK OF: _____

Exercise Ideas

Use the space below to jot down ways you would like to exercise this week. If it helps you with logistics, fill in the week below with your plans. Make sure to schedule same muscle group strength sessions on non-consecutive days and include an active rest day. Use the FITT recommendations provided in the Introduction on page 6 to guide you, but feel free to change it up based on your body and day's needs.

What I already enjoy	Cardio Ideas (3-5x/week)
1.	1.
2.	2.
3.	3.
4.	4.
5.	5.

Strength Ideas (2-3x/week)	Stretch/Mobility Ideas (2-7x/week)
1.	1.
2.	2.
3.	3.

	Sun	Mon	Tues	Wed	Thurs	Fri	Sat
What I'm Already Doing							
How I can add strength							
How I can add cardio							
How I can add mobility							

DATE: _____

Romans 10:17

"So faith comes from hearing, and hearing through the word of Christ."

Today, I'm grateful for

Time	Hunger*	What I ate	Fullness*	Satisfaction*	Notes

Fitness Felt Need*	Time	Workout	Before	After	Notes

Rate hunger, fullness and satisfaction on scale of 1-10. Reference hunger/fullness scale and fitness felt needs on pages 5-6.

Other self-care I engaged in:

Prayer:

DATE: _____

Philippians 4:8

"…[W]hatever is true, whatever is honorable, whatever is just, whatever is pure, whatever is lovely, whatever is commendable, if there is any excellence, if there is anything worthy of praise, think about these things."

Today, I'm grateful for

Time	Hunger*	What I ate	Fullness*	Satisfaction*	Notes

Fitness Felt Need*	Time	Workout	Before	After	Notes

Rate hunger, fullness and satisfaction on scale of 1-10. Reference hunger/fullness scale and fitness felt needs on pages 5-6.

Other self-care I engaged in:

Prayer:

DATE: _____

1 Timothy 4:8

"For while bodily training is of some value, godliness is of value in every way, as it holds promise for the present life and also for the life to come."

Today, I'm grateful for

Time	Hunger*	What I ate	Fullness*	Satisfaction*	Notes

Fitness Felt Need	Time	Workout	Before	After	Notes

Rate hunger, fullness and satisfaction on scale of 1-10. Reference hunger/fullness scale and fitness felt needs on pages 5-6.

Other self-care I engaged in:

Prayer:

STRENGTH EXERCISE		Date	Date	Date	Date	Date	Date
	Weight						
	Reps						
	Sets						
	RPE						
	Weight						
	Reps						
	Sets						
	RPE						
	Weight						
	Reps						
	Sets						
	RPE						
	Weight						
	Reps						
	Sets						
	RPE						
	Weight						
	Reps						
	Sets						
	RPE						
	Weight						
	Reps						
	Sets						
	RPE						
CARDIO EXERCISE		Date	Date	Date	Date	Date	Date
	Time						
	Distance						
	Intensity*						
	Time						
	Distance						
	Intensity*						

RPE: 1-10 Rate of Perceived Exertion*Intensity: L/M/V Light/Moderate/Vigorous or HR

Appendix A: Exercise Motivator Guide

Exercise Helps You Look Good: The Looker

"Put on then, as God's chosen ones, holy and beloved, compassionate hearts, kindness, humility, meekness, and patience." Colossians 3:12

You don't have to change the way you look, but exercise can help change the way you see yourself. Your body is a covering of glory, a way the Lord surrounds you with His love. That's why we call this motivator "The Looker." The Looker can shift her focus from how she looks on the outside to what God does within her by engaging in outdoor resistance training to promote serotonin, the confidence neurochemical. She'll know God sees her and loves her beyond looks.

When you need to remember what gets you going, refer to the statements below:

Looker motivation: Enjoying the Lord through exercise builds unchangeable confidence.

Joy Declaration: "I am holy, beloved, and chosen in Christ. I will lift my crown, move for joy, and walk worthy of the Lord."

Workout prayers:
- Rise above
- Hidden in Christ
- Eyes on You

Movement Ideas for the Looker:

In General:

- Wear clothes you can move in that fit you as you are
- Make it a goal to see what your body can do: set yourself a goal beyond your comfort level and strengthen your faith
- Surround yourself with inspiration, whether that's working out in an uplifting setting or being with a motivational instructor

More Specific:

- *Lift heavy:* Anaerobic weight lifting (heavier resistance training without cardio) improves confidence, rejection resistance, and resilience.
- *Get out:* Sunlight produces vitamin D which promotes serotonin production, the confidence neurochemical. Aim to get out and about for ten to thirty minutes of midday sunlight every day.
- *Recruit a friend:* If classes are intimidating, invite a close friend for confidence or hire a personal trainer to help you find your groove.

Sample 12-Week Workout Plan:

🎥 The Looker Workout Video

- 12 squats
- 12 side lunges
- 12 pushups
- 12 reverse flys
- 12 windmills
- 12 plank alternating lifts

X3

Refer to the Looker Workout Video for instruction until you can do it on your own. You're going to do this strength workout 2-3x / week on nonconsecutive days, using the workout log to track your progress. For cardio, walk or run outdoors if possible for 20+ minutes 3-5 x / week. If you would like to continue this workout plan past the 4 week mark, refer to the extended workout plan below.

Extended workout plan:

Reverse Pyramid Plan:
- Each week, take away 2 reps from each set and increase the weight by about 10%. You can increase the weight in push-ups and planks by lowering your incline from performing them on a wall to doing them on a kitchen counter, then a sofa, a step, the floor, and so forth.

Example:
- Week 1: Bodyweight x 12 reps
- Week 2: 2.5lbs x 10 reps
- Week 3: 5 lbs x 8 reps

- Week 4: 7.5 lbs x 6 reps
- Once you have completed a pyramid, you can start over with more weight:
- Week 5: 2.5lbs x 12 reps
- Week 6: 5lbs x 10 reps
- Week 7: 7.5lbs x 8 reps
- Week 8: 10 lbs x 6 reps

If you need to switch up the stimulus, create a new strength workout by subbing an exercise appropriate for that muscle group. Ex: sub chest flys for pushups.

Cardio: Each week, add speed or distance. See this sample walking / jogging plan from https://exrx.net/Aerobic/WalkProgram for specific ways to implement this.

Make it a Habit: Set Up Visual Reminders

- Take a picture of you moving for joy and save it as your phone background or profile picture. This visual cue will remind you how good exercise makes you feel and how happy you look doing it, sweat and all!
- Write, "I am chosen, holy, and beloved" on your mirrors with a dry erase marker.
- Pack your gym bag for the next day, and set it in a high traffic area so you won't miss it.
- Post your work-out schedule on your fridge.
- Set a wake-up alarm on your phone, with a prayer like: "Rise up, crown on, move in Love."

Encouragement:

Nourish your inner worth. Don't skip out on something fun that you think others would point and laugh at. Get in the front of that Jazzercise class and own those dance moves! Instead of looking to the mirror, peers, family, friends, or culture for visual approval, remember who you are and whose you are. You are holy, beloved, and chosen in Christ. He sees you and covers you with His safe love. That sense of security frees you to radiate the strength of someone who stands firm in her identity, unafraid to try hard and see what God made her body to do.

Celebrate:

If your mind wanders during your workout, celebrate the moment by reminding yourself, "eyes up," and see His face smiling back at you. When you accomplish a set goal, celebrate by doing something that makes you feel more fit in your skin, like buying new workout clothes that make you feel confident in your body.

Godly Training Transformation

You are aware of the trendy new program that promises quick visible results, but you do not have to buy into it. You're choosing to be loved by God and build up your strength in Christ. You lift more than what you thought, you join your friend in the new exercise class even if you look like a newbie, and when you look in the mirror, what you see most is not your body but a daughter of the King whose eyes are on Him. You are ultimately training a compassionate heart, kindness, humility, meekness, and patience in the Lord.

Exercise helps You De-Stress: The Freebird

"Or do you not know that your body is a temple of the Holy Spirit within you, whom you have from God?" 1 Corinthians 6:19

You can regulate stressful thoughts by getting out of your head and into your body, which is the temple of the Lord, the meeting place of God! The Freebird finds her joy in fitness by inviting God to be with her as she goes on outdoor adventures, does barefoot yoga, or moves to her own beat, regulating her parasympathetic nervous system to restore the internal peace. Where the Spirit of the Lord is, there is a Freebird.

When you need to remember what gets you going, refer to the statements below:

Freebird motivation: Enjoying the Lord through exercise *is* freedom.

Joy declaration: "I am a temple of the Holy Spirit. I will move for joy to meet God right where I am and find peace."

Workout prayers:
- Inhale "Jesus," exhale "sets me free"
- "I'm with You, You're with Me"
- "In step with the Spirit"

Movement Ideas for the Freebird

In General:

- You are carried through the workout with rhythm, whether that's moving through inhales and exhales, or drumming to the beat of the music.
- Allow for creativity.
- Monitor or count your breath instead using of a timer.

More Specific:

- Ground your live wires: in the event of a wayward mood, try grounding your joy circuit with the following mindfulness exercises:
    - Overlap your hands together and press them over your heart to feel the beat. Start walking to the beat of your heart and feel how it adapts, reminding you that you can adapt, too.
    - Walk barefoot in the grass.
    - Awaken your whole body by extending and flexing each joint, starting with your feet all the way up to your head.
- Interior retreat: Choose any form of retreat, whether that's into your mind like yoga, breathing meditation, or losing yourself to the rhythm of dancing.
- Exterior retreat: Get outside of your environment like going for a walk, run, hike, bike, or other outdoor activity.

12-Week Sample Freebird Plan

Consistency is key. Instead of making yourself a rigid plan that you'll never want to use, use the monthly calendars provided and circle the days you're planning on exercising. If you need a recipe to start with, refer to the Freebird Exercise video. Once you move that day, fill in the circle with the facial expression of how you felt afterwards so you can make a practice of seeing the whole picture at the end of the month. Make a consistency goal of committing to a certain number of workouts a week, modifying the length or intensity of the workout whenever you need to, but making sure you show up consistently.

Use the FITT guide on page 6 to plan your workouts each week.

Be Aware of These Stumbling Stones:

- *Do you get too much variety and need to create structure?* Buckle down and do the Looker or the Hero workout twice a week.
- *Do you do the same thing every day?* Make it a point to balance out your cardio and strength. To add strength, add small weights to your cardio routine or add two strength days. Add cardio by taking out rest between strength sets and adding an element of speed to your strength sets for a power cardio boost.

Make it a Habit: Get Centered

- *Use your breath:* Try this breath after you workout to train the stress-relaxation response. Breathe in through your nostrils to 50 percent of your lung capacity, then another breath to 80 percent, then a third breath to fill your lungs and expand your diaphragm. Release through a long exhale, feeling a dropping sensation below your navel and pausing at the bottom. Do it during a stress trigger, like being stuck in traffic or in the middle of an argument. Repeat and imagine God's presence filling your lungs until you feel more at peace.
- *Exhale longer:* When in stress, practice exhaling longer than you inhale to establish a sense of safety.
- *Feel your feet on the ground:* Anxiety pulls you apart, so recruit physical sensations to integrate your body. As you feel the ground underneath you, let it be a reminder of your anchored location: this is where you are, and this is where you start. The Lord is here.
- *Anchor any loose plans with a schedule:* Plan your workouts at the beginning of each week so there are no unknowns, and consider using a paper planner to avoid digital distractions.
- *Add on to movements that already bring you joy:* For example, if you love to dance and need to add muscular strength, consider adding light hand weights to every other dance session.

Encouragement:

You don't need to escape your life to feel freedom. You are a temple of the Holy Spirit, who makes you whole right where you. Don't mistake responsibility for a prison, and sulk inside because you are an adult and need to clean the house. Use your Freebird creativity to make cleaning into an exercise game! You already have everything you need to keep your body fit, you just might need to ask for the Lord to open the eyes of your heart and see His abundance of avenues. Make it a point to regularly meet with God in the space of your body and find the freedom of peace, so you can help others find that same joy of contentment.

Celebrate:

When your mind wanders during your workout, bring your awareness back to the Lord by saying, "You're with me." When you complete your consistency goal at the end of each month or season, consider celebrating by splurging on a new class or investing in the activity you already love doing, like a new pair of running shoes or purchasing a state park pass to give yourself permission to hike more.

Godly Training Transformation: What Freebird Maturity Looks Like

You don't let distractions pull you away from what the Lord knows is best for you. You pay less attention to your comfort on the couch or in a rigid routine, and care more about feeling comforted by the presence of the Lord, whether that means Him calling you out on an energizing walk, or to take a break from workouts. You delight in developing long-term character development rather than short-term feel-good movements because you'd rather be with God than anywhere else. You'll follow Him anywhere! You are training your spirit to have open eyes, ears, and a heart to understand that the Lord is always with you.

Exercise Helps You Be Fit and Ready: The Hero

"Therefore, if anyone cleanses himself from what is dishonorable, he will be a vessel for honorable use, set apart as holy, useful to the master of the house, ready for every good work." Timothy 2:21

The Hero is motivated to exercise by making herself ready and fit for whatever the day will bring her, whether that's the stress of a high-performance job or getting to wrestle a toddler into his car seat. Since her body is God's vessel, she finds joy in fitness by asking the Lord to fill her up with the joy of His strength. Short, effective workouts like timed intervals with compound movements release adrenaline, the energy neurochemical she needs to keep going. She'll be reminded that Christ is the Hero working through her.

When you need to remember what gets you going, refer to the statements below:

Hero motivation: Enjoying the Lord through exercise equips you for every good work.

Joy declaration: I will move for joy and be filled with energy to advance the Kingdom.

Workout prayers:
- "Your joy, my strength"
- "Empty the tank, fill the heart"
- "Ready for every good work"

Movement Ideas for the Hero:

In general:

- Perform compound exercises
- Do workout intervals within a set timeframe
- Use a timer to keep yourself on track

More specific:

- *Variety of movement:* For a creativity boost, add in linear, multiplanar, and cross-directional exercises to bridge both sides of the brain and integrate imaginative thought with executive strategy. For an example of each, try performing a forward lunge (linear), side lunge (multiplanar), and curtsy lunge (cross-directional). Do movements like these within three hours of a creative endeavor for the most effective results. See examples in your exercise video.
- *Move for more brain cells*: Exercise, in all forms, can stimulate something called BDNF in our brains. It stands for Brain Derived Neurotrophic Factor. This protein promotes the survival of nerve cells (neurons) by playing a role in the growth, maturation (differentiation), and maintenance of these cells. Exercise at sixty to seventy percent of your heart rate for twenty to thirty minutes before a big meeting or learning course to expand your capacity to take in and apply new information.
- *Submaximal output:* Moderate levels of walking, interval training, Pilates, spinning, and bodyweight strength exercises are bound to increase energy without leaving you feeling depleted afterwards.

Understand the Specific Adaptation to Imposed Demands (SAID) principle: Your body will meet the demand you give it. Don't be afraid to set a goal and see how your strength will rise to meet it.

Sample 12-Week Hero Plan

📷 The Hero Workout Video

Perform each exercise for 20 seconds at a high intensity, and rest for 10 seconds in between exercises:

3-10 minute warm-up (older and less-trained individuals need a longer warm-up)
- Forward and backward curtsy lunges
- Quick feet drops

X2
20 second rest

- Cat walks
- Lateral jumps

X2
20 second rest

- Rocketship pushups
- Running punches

X2
20 second rest

- Renegade rows
- Weighted skaters

x2
20 second rest

- Lunge, serve the platter
- Superman to tuck jump

X2
20 second rest

- Thread the needle planks
- Cross jacks

X2
20 second rest

3-10 minute cool-down

Do the Hero Workout Video (as written above) 2-3x a week on nonconsecutive days. Every week or two, experiment with increasing the weight you use for the workouts by 10% and / or count your reps for each exercise and see if you can increase them each week at a safe pace, using full range of motion. Use the workout log to chart your progress each week.

If you would like to change it up after the first month, try the Looker strength workout once or twice a week. Make sure to get in a strength workout at least 2x / week.
Go for leisurely walks as often as you can to explore, get out of your head, and enjoy creation. Make sure to journal in your weekly log about how you feel afterwards.

Make it a Habit: Focus on Being Filled

- *Find your uninterrupted time:* Figure out when you can work out without any interruptions. It could be early in the morning before it's socially appropriate to send email, or at night when everyone is winding down and the kids are asleep.
- *Block out your workouts as warm-ups:* As you set appointments to take care of business, schedule a workout that will support the business of your day, whether that be a corporate meeting or a parenting play date. Consider your workout as a work warm-up, a non-negotiable schedule block that feeds the rest of your day.
- *Celebrate work milestones in your day by taking a movement break:* For example, set a timer to work for forty-five minutes and do a yoga sequence for an active break, or celebrate 5 p.m. or the end of your work day with a mini dance party.
- *Use timers as boundary lines:* Set a timer at the start of your workout so you know exactly how long you have and can fill up the time efficiently.

Encouragement:

Don't try to fix everyone and everything before you do something fun. Leave the house a mess and take the crying kids outside for a water balloon fight. Leave the email pile and go explore a new area of the office. Don't work harder, seek the Kingdom! Everything else, including your body, will fall into line when God is foremost. Know what's yours to own for the day, and only do the activity you need to support those priorities. If you want to do more, great! Let it be done in the strength of His joy.

Celebrate:

When you're working out, don't focus on what still needs to be done, how long this workout is going to last, or what else you could be doing. Remember what God has already done for you, and striving will fall by the wayside. Become a participant in what He is doing now by allowing yourself to be present in the moment and proclaim in prayer: "You're enough for me!" Celebrate the end of your goal by doing something related to self-care as a way to treat yourself as His daughter who loves you. It could be as simple as rewarding yourself with a hot bath and a good book, or as extravagant as planning a spa day for you and a friend, sister, or daughter.

Godly Training Transformation

You're not afraid of a workout, because you know it can be a tool to give you more energy. Every time you exercise, you are practicing self-emptying and God-filling. You are not a slave to time, and know good things take time. Carving out a time for exercise feels less like an anxious "I don't have time for this!" kind of task but one that produces the lasting fruit of patience. You know you're building within a Kingdom that will last. You're training holiness, perseverance, and dedication to the Lord and His good work. Whenever you begin to feel burdened with fitness expectations, you will give up your concern in prayer, let Him take the yoke, and find rest for your soul.

Exercise Helps You Feel Alive: The Warrior

"Instead, speaking the truth in love, we will grow to become in every respect the mature body of him who is the head, that is, Christ. From him the whole body, joined and held together by every supporting ligament, grows and builds itself up in love, as each part does its work." Ephesians 4:15-16

The Warrior knows she is not alone, but part of the body of Christ. She is motivated to workout when faced with a challenge, especially if it includes other people. She yearns to experience the collective victory her spirit already knows in Christ. The Warrior finds joy in fitness when she invites someone else into a specific competitive goal like a race, a sport, or to help her break a personal record. This releases dopamine and oxytocin so the Warrior can feel both accomplished and connected in Christ.

When you need to remember what gets you going, refer to the statements below:

Warrior motivation: Enjoying the Lord through exercise *is* to walk in victory.

Joy Declaration: "I will build up the body of Christ by giving my best and connecting with others in the joy of movement."

Workout prayers:
- "In this together"
- "His love never quits"
- "Celebrate!"

Movement Ideas for the Warrior:

In general:

- Set SMART goals
- Find your flow: know your aim, get constant feedback, and adjust the challenge to fit your ability
- Invite a friend or join a group program to compete with

More specific:

- *Set and achieve a goal*: The Warrior seeks the accomplished effects of dopamine. Go into every workout with a specific goal to reach, whether that be a time to beat, a mindfulness activity to focus on, or a certain number of exercises to complete. Consider joining a thirty-day challenge or trying a gym with built-in competition, like heart rate monitoring or performance posts. Make sure you remember that you're not working *against* anyone but *with* each other!

- *Exercise with someone:* Make a point to work out in the physical presence others, whether that be joining a running club, simply going to a gym where others are working out, or at home with a neighbor. These activities are shown to release oxytocin so you can experience human connection and feel connected with the body of Christ.
- *Get out of your comfort zone:* For a surge of adrenaline to make you feel more alive, do something a little out of the ordinary for you. Hike a new location, try a different fitness studio, join a sports team, or sign up for a skill-specific series like boxing or karate.
- *Join the kids*: If you're a parent whose kid is involved in a sport that offers classes or teams for adults, get in on the fun and try it out. They might even offer a family discount!

Sample 12-Week Workout Plan:

🎥 The Warrior Exercise Video

50s workout: Perform 10 reps of each exercise

Set 1:

- Squats
- Pushups
- Burpees
- Supermans
- Plank jacks

Set 2 (Wide)

Set 3 (Narrow)

Set 4 (Alternate legs)

Set 5 (Power up)

You may choose to do this workout 2-3 times a week on nonconsecutive days, and add 3-5 days of cardio if you don't get your heart pumping enough. Add 10% weight each week or two to continue progressing the workouts.

The above workout from the video is one example of a workout challenge. Make your challenge fit you! Sign up for an in-person or digital fitness challenge at the end of your 12 weeks.

Here are a few ideas in order of least to greatest difficulty, but I recommend you pick the movement challenge that gives you joy. If you love to dance, host a 12-hour dance marathon for charity; if you want to master a handstand, take a local gymnastics class or ask a yoga teacher to tutor you; if you love Crossfit, commit to a WOD challenge. If you want stronger arms, do push-ups or practice pull-ups every day for 30 days. Here are some other ideas:

- **Walking and running**: Couch to 5K: Revelation Wellness has an excellent Couch to 5K program that weaves faith into the training plan. Or you may choose to create your own distance or speed goal.
- **Pick your strength:** Choose one area from the fitness test from Week 2 you would like to specifically improve upon.
- **Military Basic Training Test:** Try out the army's physical fitness test by doing two minutes of push-ups, two minutes of sit-ups, and a timed 2-mile run. Perform as many repetitions as possible and your two miles as fast as possible, all within a safe range of motion.

I am committing to:

My training plan is to complete these goals each week:

Week 12:

Week 11:

Week 10:

Week 9:

Week 8:

Week 7:

Week 6:

Week 5:

Week 4:

Week 3:

Week 2:

Week 1:

My weekly exercise plan I will change out weekly in pencil:

Sun	Mon	Tues	Wed	Thurs	Friday	Sat

Notes:

Make It A Habit: Invite others

- Have a standing weekly workout appointment you can invite others to, like a run outside or a class at the gym.
- Check in with your workout buddy on a set weekly time.
- Use operant conditioning by setting up one goal to complete each week, like challenging yourself to add in an exercise session, or attempting a higher box jump.
- Grab a friend and sign up for a race together, or sign up alone and find another participant in the race to train with.
- Challenge someone to a steps competition with a fitness tracker. Set the tracker to remind you when you need to get in extra steps.

Encouragement:

Use your imagination to turn ordinary movements into extraordinary feats. Imagine your mountain climbers are helping you get up Mount Everest, visualize competing against Tour de France cyclists while on a spin bike, take down the fictional boxing opponent in the ring while throwing punches on a bag. The Warrior also loves company, but don't be discouraged from fitness if you can't get a whole soccer team together to play. Just find one other person. Two and the Lord is an army!

Celebrate:

The Warrior celebrates in the middle of her workout by proclaiming, "Your love doesn't quit," even when it's hard and she wants to give up. She knows that no matter what, His strength and victory is hers. To celebrate a big milestone, the Warrior would most enjoy a fun time with friends, like signing up for a big race or new workout class and going out for smoothies afterwards.

Godly Transformation Training

Just because you failed to finish a program, your team lost or your workout was just a walk around the block, you no longer feel like you've lost. You know that when you're with Christ, you have already won. You are aware that pride comes before a fall, but the humble are honored. You take joy in serving others first, whether that's setting out weights for a friend in class or inviting them to workout with you. And even if nobody can join you, Jesus is enough company! You're training maturity in love for the building up of Christ's whole body.

Exercise Helps You Feel Better: The Keeper

"So we make it our goal to please him, whether we are at home in the body or away from it."
2 Corinthians 5:9, NIV

The Keeper is motivated to exercise because she knows it's a wise investment into her long-term health—acting as a good steward to keep the one home God has given her for life. She finds joy in fitness by devoting her workout to God as a way to express thanksgiving for her good body. The best exercise for The Keeper is sustainable, consistent, and releases serotonin, like completing 10,000 steps per day, biking to work, or waking up with stretches and calisthenics. She knows that in Christ, she is a Keeper.

When you need to remember what gets you going, refer to the statements below:

Keeper motivation: Enjoying the Lord through the gift of exercise *is* good stewardship.

Joy declaration: "I will show reverence for the Lord by respecting my body through a lifetime of joy-filled exercise with Him."

Workout prayers:
- "All for the Lord"
- "Finish strong"
"Faithful to the end"

Movement Ideas for the Keeper

In General:

- Think of your whole day as movement
- Wear clothes you can move in for every occasion
- Find a healthcare professional you trust for guidance

More Specific:

- *Moderate-intensity aerobic exercise:* One-hundred fifty minutes per week (about thirty minutes, five days a week) of aerobic exercise may slow down the aging of cells in addition to benefiting the cardiovascular system. Include cycling, swimming, or speed walking into your day at a pace which makes it harder to hold a conversation, or fifty to seventy percent of your maximum heart rate (approximately 220 minus your age).
- *Change your environment:* Make your surroundings suitable for natural movement. Put the most used items in harder-to-reach places, and reduce the use of technology.
- *Be all-inclusive:* In addition to aerobic exercise, add resistance training for bone strength. Include major movement patterns like push, pull, hinge, squat, and carry. You may do these with little to no break in between, which would count as anaerobic training and improves stamina and speeds fat loss.

Sample 12-Week Workout Plan

The Keeper Exercise Video

Ground force flow:
- Ankle rolls
- S arms
- Half get-ups
- Ab scissors
- Squats around the world
- Floor rolls
- Crab walks
- Bear crawls
- Back rolls
- Plank down dogs

Get-ups

Glider strength and cardio (10 reps each):

- Mountain climbers
- Inch worm to pushup
- Lunge switch kicks
- Bird dog extensions

Squat jacks

Floor angel crunches

- Tick tock squats
- Side plank + front leg slides

x2-3

Do this workout 2-3x per week on nonconsecutive days. Try it out with just your bodyweight, and if you want to improve on your muscular strength, add weights until you feel very challenged but can still complete the reps. Then increase around 10% each week, or go up to the next weight category, like 5lbs to 7.5 lbs.

Maintain your movement by getting in 10,000 steps a day. Improve your cardiovascular system by seeing how many rounds of 10 reps you can get in your designated time frame of working out. Always focus on safe form and speed. No injuries allowed! Start with a 20-minute workout, but if you have more time some days, feel free to try and get in more rounds. Use the workout log to chart your progress.

You may choose to do the Looker, Freebird, or Hero workout one of your days, just make sure to do this workout once a week so you can see your progress at the end.

Make it a Habit: Build Reminders into Your Regular Routine

- If getting up is hard but it's your only time to workout, you could try wearing your workout clothes for pajamas to make getting morning exercise a no-brainer. If you're a parent, consider wearing athleisure clothes as your wardrobe so you'll be ready to move at all times.
- When getting ready for work, pack yourself a gym bag in addition to a lunch. Keep an extra gym bag in the car in case you forget something.
- During your workouts, set up interval timers with a pleasant ding as a reminder to celebrate short finish lines.
- Install a pull-up bar in a doorway and do one (or a twenty-second hang) when you pass through, or during certain times of the day.
- Put up an old-fashioned reward chart on your fridge, complete with star stickers.
- Hire a personal trainer to text you friendly reminders to move throughout the week.

Encouragement

It's okay if you don't have a perfect plan—just get your tennis shoes on, go outside, and figure out what feels good to you. By remembering that Christ is your righteousness, you're doing it right. If you can't remember what's fun, think about what you liked to do as a kid or what you would do if you had a free day. Enjoying exercise is not frivolous, but reduces stress, prolongs your life, and makes it feel worth living!

Celebrate

The Keeper doesn't have to wait to accomplish a workout before she can celebrate. She can enjoy God's presence right in the middle of exercising, perhaps when she is exerting the most effort, by praising Him and saying, "You approve!" because He already does. Consider marking the end of your 12 weeks with a new planner, a fancy fitness app, hiring a trainer, or purchasing a course for even better stewardship and enjoyment with the Lord.

Godly Transformation Training

You're no longer trying to win approval of your health professional by shedding pounds or exercising only under the fear of avoiding disease. Now, you see yourself walking in Christ's righteousness, and take joy in obeying the Lord wholeheartedly in the small moments of the day, whether that is holding a plank 10 seconds more or even less than the plan requires. You know that the Lord sees it all, keeps close accounts, and treasures every act of faith as you walk with Him. You're training His faithfulness, and He is always faithful!

Acknowledgments

*"Trust in the LORD with all your heart,
and do not lean on your own understanding.
In all your ways acknowledge him,
and he will make straight your paths."*
Proverbs 3:5-6

First and foremost, Jesus, we thank you for freeing us from ourselves and walking with us on this path of true health with you! We are thankful to our clients who have inspired us, and our families who have supported us. We could not have made this happen without the help of these very wonderful people. Thank you to GG and Papa Golbek, Grandma and Papaw Hertzler, Yia Yia and Papa Daniel, and Grandpa and Nanny Bandy for watching our children while we created this course. A huge shout out to our husbands, Dwayne Golbek and Mattox Shuler for all course videography, photography, and book cover design.

About the Authors

Aubrey Golbek is a writer, dietitian, and mom with a passion for God's Word and food freedom. Aubrey is the author of *Grace, Food, and Everything in Between.* She owns Grace Fueled Nutrition, a private nutrition counseling practice with the mission to help women ditch shame and find grace with food, body image, and motherhood. Aubrey lives in Tulsa, OK with her husband and children. You can connect with Aubrey at gracefueled.com or on Instagram @gracefueled_rd

Kasey Shuler is the author of *Move For Joy* and several bible studies, including *The Lord's Prayer: A 12-Week Journal, Rest and Rise,* and *Love Beyond Looks*. Working with clients as an ACSM personal trainer and Revelation Wellness fitness instructor, Kasey's mission is to help go-getters discover how God is with us, body and spirit. She lives with her husband and two daughters in Athens, Georgia, and would love to connect with you at kaseybshuler.com or on Instagram @kaseybshuler.

Made in the USA
Coppell, TX
04 October 2024